SALZBURG

TRAVEL GUIDE

2024 2025

Discover the Magic of Mozart's City
Insider Tips, Hidden Gems, Must-See
Attractions and Unforgettable Experiences
for Your First Austrian Adventure

DIANE F. THOMPSON

Copyright © by DIANE F. THOMPSON

All rights reserved. This book and its contents are protected under the copyright laws of the United States and other countries. No part of this publication may be reproduced, distributed, or transmitted in any form or by any means, including photocopying, recording, or other electronic or mechanical methods, without the prior written permission of the author, except in the case of brief quotations embodied in critical reviews and certain other non - commercial uses permitted by copyright law.

The information contained in this book is provided for informational purposes only. The author and publisher make no representations or warranties regarding the accuracy or completeness of the contents of this book. The views and opinions expressed in the book are those of the author and do not necessarily reflect the official policy or position of any organization or individual

FORWARD

Salzburg, a city where music dances on the air and history whispers from ancient stones, awaits your discovery. Within these pages lies a gateway to its timeless allure – a carefully crafted guide to unlock its hidden gems, immerse yourself in its vibrant culture, and embrace the spirit of Mozart's birthplace.

Whether you're drawn to iconic landmarks, scenic trails, or culinary delights, this book is your compass, leading you on an unforgettable journey through Salzburg's heart and soul. Let its melodies, its landscapes, and its people inspire you, as you create your own unique Salzburg story.

May this guide be your key to unlocking the magic of Mozart's city.
Happy travels!

MAP OF SALZBURG

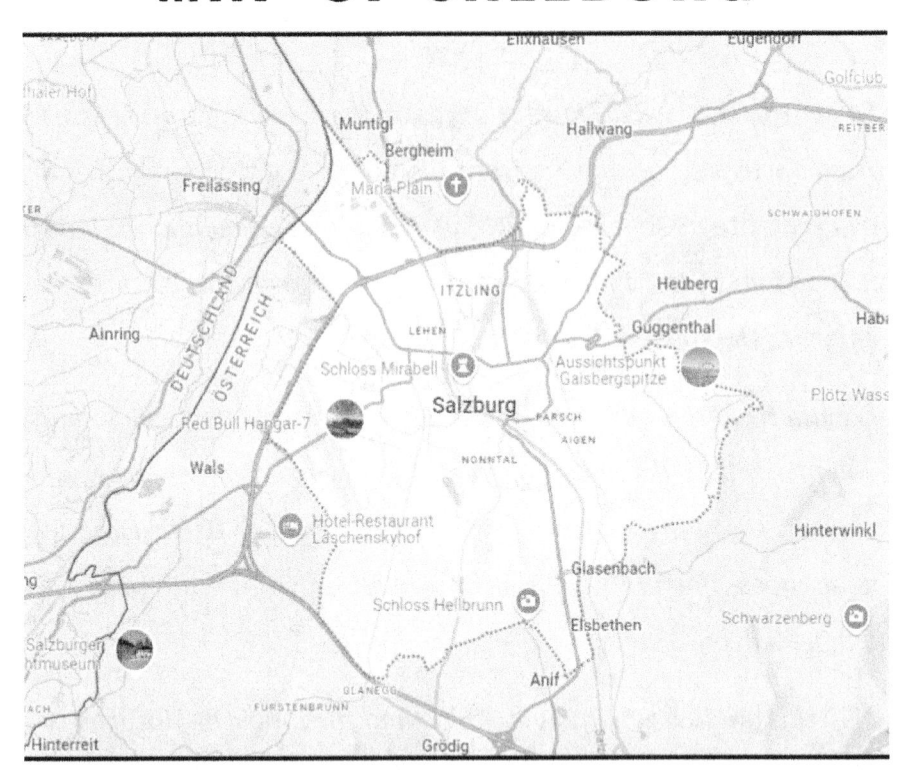

HOW TO SCAN THE CODE

1. Open the camera app on your device.
2. Place the QR code inside the camera frame.
3. Wait for your device to recognize the QR code.
4. Follow the prompts that appear.
5. Take action based on the scanned content.

4 | SALZBURG TRAVEL GUIDE 2025

5 | SALZBURG TRAVEL GUIDE 2025

6 | SALZBURG TRAVEL GUIDE 2025

7 | SALZBURG TRAVEL GUIDE 2025

CONTENTS

INTRODUCTION 12

  Welcome to Salzburg... 12

    Brief history and cultural context 13

    Setting expectations 15

CHAPTER 1 20

  Planning Your Trip 20

    Best Time to Visit 20

    Getting to Salzburg 24

    Visas and Entry Requirements 29

    Accommodation Options 32

    Packing Essentials 37

CHAPTER 2 43

  Salzburg's Must-See Landmarks 43

    Hohensalzburg Fortress 43

    Salzburg Cathedral 46

    Mirabell Palace and Gardens 52

    Mozart's Birthplace and Residence 55

Getreidegasse 59

CHAPTER 3 65

Salzburg's Hidden Gems 65

Mönchsberg 65

Hellbrunn Palace and Trick Fountains 69

St. Peter's Abbey and Cemetery 72

Salzburg Museum 75

Residenzplatz and the Salzburg Residenz 78

CHAPTER 4 84

Experiencing Salzburg's Culture 84

Salzburg Festival 84

Mozart Week 88

Salzburg Marionette Theatre 91

Local Markets and Festivals 95

Traditional Austrian Cuisine 98

CHAPTER 5 105

Exploring Salzburg's Surroundings 105

Day Trip to Hallstatt 105

Eagle's Nest and the Bavarian Alps 109

Sound of Music Tour 112

Salzburg Lake District 115

Berchtesgaden National Park 119

CHAPTER 6 .... **125**

Practical Tips for First-Time Travelers **125**

Getting Around Salzburg 125

Money and Currency Exchange 128

Safety and Security 132

Local Customs and Etiquette 135

Language Basics 138

CHAPTER 7 .... **145**

Salzburg for Specific Interests **145**

Salzburg for Families 145

Salzburg for Couples 149

Salzburg for Solo Travelers 154

Salzburg for Budget Travelers 158

Salzburg for Luxury Travelers 162

CHAPTER 8 .... **170**

Salzburg Itineraries **170**

3-Day Itinerary 170

5-Day Itinerary 174

7-Day Itinerary 180

Themed Itineraries 184

CHAPTER 9 189

Salzburg Off the Beaten Path 189

Non-Touristy Neighborhoods 189

Lesser-Known Museums and Galleries 193

Local Events and Festivals 198

Hiking and Biking Trails 202

Day Trips to Hidden Gems 206

CHAPTER 10 211

Salzburg Travel Resources 211

Useful Websites and Apps 211

Local Tour Operators and Guides 215

Emergency Contact Information 220

Additional Tips and Advice 223

CONCLUSION 229

Reflect on the magic of Salzburg 229

Encourage exploration and discovery 230

Final tips and farewell 232

INTRODUCTION

Welcome to Salzburg

Nestled amidst the breathtaking scenery of the Austrian Alps, Salzburg is a city that effortlessly blends history, culture, and natural beauty. Known as the birthplace of the legendary composer Wolfgang Amadeus Mozart, Salzburg resonates with the echoes of his music and the spirit of his genius. As you wander through its cobblestone streets and gaze upon its Baroque masterpieces, you'll be transported to a world where time seems to stand still.

Salzburg is a feast for the senses. Its historic center, a UNESCO World Heritage Site, is a treasure trove of architectural wonders, from the imposing Hohensalzburg Fortress to the graceful Mirabell Palace. The city's vibrant cultural scene offers a symphony of experiences, from the world-renowned Salzburg Festival to intimate concerts in Mozart's birthplace. And for those seeking outdoor adventures, the surrounding mountains and lakes beckon with opportunities for hiking, biking, and skiing.

Whether you're a music lover, a history buff, or simply someone who appreciates beauty and charm, Salzburg has something to offer. This guidebook is designed to help first-time travelers navigate the city with confidence, offering insider tips, practical advice, and recommendations for unforgettable experiences. From iconic landmarks to hidden gems, from traditional cuisine to contemporary culture, we'll guide you through the heart and soul of Salzburg.

Prepare to be enchanted by Salzburg's timeless allure. As you stroll through its picturesque streets, listen to the strains of Mozart's music, and savor the flavors of Austrian cuisine, you'll discover why this city is a true gem of Europe. Whether you're seeking a romantic getaway, a family adventure, or a solo exploration, Salzburg promises to leave a lasting impression on your heart and soul.

So, open your heart to the magic of Salzburg. Let its music, its history, and its natural beauty weave their spell upon you. This is a city that invites you to slow down, to savor the moment, and to create memories that will last a lifetime. Welcome to Salzburg, where dreams and reality intertwine.

Brief history and cultural context

Salzburg's story unfolds across centuries, leaving an indelible mark on its present-day character. The city's roots trace back to Roman times, when it was known as Iuvavum, a thriving settlement along the Salzach River. Its strategic location and abundant salt deposits (Salz means "salt" in German) fueled its growth and prosperity.

During the Middle Ages, Salzburg emerged as a powerful ecclesiastical principality, ruled by prince-archbishops who wielded both spiritual and secular authority. Their ambition and patronage transformed Salzburg into a cultural and artistic hub, attracting renowned architects, sculptors, and musicians.

The Baroque era, spanning the 17th and 18th centuries, marked Salzburg's golden age. The prince-archbishops embarked on ambitious building projects, adorning the city with magnificent palaces, churches, and squares. The Italian architect Vincenzo Scamozzi, known for his work on St. Mark's Square in Venice, left his mark on Salzburg with the design of the Salzburg Cathedral.

It was during this period that Salzburg's most famous son, Wolfgang Amadeus Mozart, was born in 1756. His extraordinary musical talent blossomed in the city's vibrant cultural atmosphere, and his legacy continues to resonate through its streets and concert halls. Today, Mozart's birthplace and residence are popular pilgrimage sites for music lovers from around the world.

Salzburg's Baroque architectural heritage is a testament to its rich history and cultural significance. The city's skyline is dominated by the imposing Hohensalzburg Fortress, a medieval stronghold that offers breathtaking views of the surrounding landscape. The Salzburg Cathedral, with its majestic dome and ornate facade, is a masterpiece of Baroque design. And the Mirabell Palace, with its elegant gardens and iconic Pegasus Fountain, is a reminder of the city's princely past.

Salzburg's cultural landscape is equally vibrant. The annual Salzburg Festival, founded in 1920, is a world-renowned celebration of music, theater, and opera. Mozart Week, held each January, pays homage to the city's most famous son with a series of concerts and events. And throughout the year, Salzburg's theaters, concert halls, and museums offer a diverse range of cultural experiences.

As you explore Salzburg, you'll encounter a harmonious blend of history, culture, and artistic expression. Its Baroque architecture, its musical heritage, and its natural beauty create an ambiance that is both captivating and inspiring. Salzburg is a city that invites you to immerse yourself in its rich tapestry, to discover its hidden treasures, and to create your own unforgettable memories.

Setting expectations

As you embark on your journey to Salzburg, prepare to be captivated by a symphony of experiences that will resonate long after you've left. This city, with its harmonious blend of history, culture, and natural beauty, offers a feast for the senses and a treasure trove of memories waiting to be made.

From the moment you arrive, you'll be greeted by a visual spectacle. The city's skyline, dominated by the imposing Hohensalzburg Fortress, sets the stage for an adventure steeped in history and grandeur. As you wander through the UNESCO-listed Old Town, you'll be transported back in time, surrounded by Baroque masterpieces that whisper tales of a bygone era. The Salzburg Cathedral, with its majestic dome and intricate facade, will leave you breathless, while the Mirabell Palace and its enchanting gardens will inspire dreams of waltzing princesses and fairytale romances.

But Salzburg is more than just a collection of landmarks. It's a living, breathing city with a vibrant cultural scene that pulsates with energy. The sounds of Mozart's music fill the air, from street performers serenading passersby to world-class concerts in historic venues. The Salzburg Festival, a highlight of the cultural calendar, attracts artists and audiences from around the globe, offering a feast of opera, theater, and classical music.

Beyond the city center, hidden gems await discovery. Wander through the charming streets of the Nonntal district, where traditional houses and hidden courtyards offer a glimpse into local life. Climb the Mönchsberg for panoramic views of the city and the surrounding mountains, or explore the whimsical Hellbrunn Palace and its playful trick fountains.

Salzburg's culinary scene is equally enticing. Indulge in traditional Austrian dishes like Wiener Schnitzel and Tafelspitz, or savor the delicate flavors of Salzburger Nockerl, a fluffy soufflé that melts in your mouth. And don't forget to sample the city's signature treat, Mozartkugeln, chocolate marzipan balls that are as delightful as they are delicious.

For those seeking outdoor adventures, Salzburg's surroundings offer endless possibilities. Hike through the breathtaking scenery of the Salzkammergut Lake District, or take a scenic boat ride on the Wolfgangsee. In winter, the nearby ski resorts beckon with powdery slopes and cozy mountain huts.

Whether you're a music lover, a history buff, a foodie, or an outdoor enthusiast, Salzburg has something to offer. This guidebook will help you navigate the city's many attractions, offering insider tips, practical advice, and recommendations for unforgettable experiences. From iconic landmarks to hidden gems, from traditional cuisine to contemporary culture, we'll guide you through the heart and soul of Salzburg.

So, open your heart to the magic of Salzburg. Let its music, its history, and its natural beauty weave their spell upon you. This is a city that invites you to slow down, to savor the moment, and to create memories that will last a lifetime. Welcome to Salzburg, where dreams and reality intertwine. Your Austrian adventure awaits!

19 | SALZBURG TRAVEL GUIDE 2025

CHAPTER 1

Planning Your Trip

Best Time to Visit

Choosing the ideal time to visit Salzburg depends largely on your preferences and priorities. Each season paints the city in a different light, offering unique experiences and considerations for travelers.

Spring (March-May)

- **Advantages:**
    - Mild temperatures: Spring brings pleasant weather, with average highs ranging from 10°C to 20°C (50°F to 68°F).
    - Blooming flowers: The city's parks and gardens come alive with vibrant colors, creating a picturesque backdrop for your explorations.
    - Fewer crowds: Compared to the peak summer season, spring sees fewer tourists, allowing for a more relaxed and intimate experience.

- o Easter Festival: This prestigious classical music festival takes place during Holy Week, offering a unique cultural experience.

- **Disadvantages:**
  - o Unpredictable weather: Spring can be fickle, with occasional rain showers and cooler temperatures.
  - o Limited outdoor activities: Some mountain trails and outdoor attractions may still be closed due to snow or muddy conditions.

Summer (June-August)

- **Advantages:**
  - o Warm and sunny weather: Summer offers ideal conditions for outdoor activities, with average highs reaching 25°C (77°F).
  - o Long daylight hours: Enjoy extended daylight, allowing for more time to explore the city and its surroundings.
  - o Salzburg Festival: This world-renowned festival takes place in July and August, attracting top-tier performers and cultural enthusiasts.
  - o Vibrant atmosphere: The city comes alive with outdoor cafes, street performers, and a lively energy.

- **Disadvantages:**
    - Peak season crowds: Summer is the busiest time to visit Salzburg, so expect larger crowds and higher prices for accommodations.
    - Limited availability: Booking accommodations and tours well in advance is essential during this peak season.

Autumn (September-November)

- **Advantages:**
    - Comfortable temperatures: Autumn brings a pleasant chill to the air, with average highs ranging from 15°C to 5°C (59°F to 41°F).
    - Colorful foliage: The surrounding mountains transform into a tapestry of reds, oranges, and yellows, creating stunning scenery.
    - Fewer crowds: As the peak season subsides, crowds thin out, offering a more tranquil experience.
    - Cultural events: The Mozart Week festival takes place in late January, celebrating the composer's birthday with concerts and events.

- **Disadvantages:**

- Shorter daylight hours: As winter approaches, daylight decreases, limiting time for outdoor activities.
- Some attractions close: Certain outdoor attractions and mountain trails may close for the season as temperatures drop.

Winter (December-February)

- **Advantages:**
  - Festive atmosphere: Salzburg transforms into a winter wonderland during the Christmas season, with charming markets and twinkling lights.
  - Winter sports: The surrounding mountains offer opportunities for skiing, snowboarding, and other winter activities.
  - Fewer crowds: Winter sees fewer tourists, allowing for a more peaceful and intimate experience.

- **Disadvantages:**
  - Cold temperatures: Winter can be quite cold, with average lows dipping below freezing.
  - Limited daylight: Daylight hours are short, requiring careful planning for outdoor activities.

- - Some attractions close: Certain outdoor attractions and boat tours may be unavailable during the winter months.

Recommendations for First-Time Travelers:

- **Shoulder seasons (spring or autumn) are ideal:** These seasons offer pleasant weather, fewer crowds, and a good balance of indoor and outdoor activities.

- **Summer is perfect for outdoor enthusiasts:** If you enjoy warm weather and long days, summer is a great time to visit, but be prepared for larger crowds.

- **Winter offers a festive charm:** If you love Christmas markets and winter sports, consider a visit during the holiday season.

Ultimately, the best time to visit Salzburg depends on your personal preferences and interests. Consider the weather, crowds, festivals, and activities that appeal to you most when making your decision. With careful planning, you can experience the magic of Salzburg in any season.

Getting to Salzburg

Salzburg, nestled amidst the Austrian Alps, is a well-connected city easily accessible via air, rail, and road. Let's explore the diverse transportation options that can seamlessly transport you to this enchanting destination:

By Air

- **Salzburg Airport (SZG)**: The most convenient and time-efficient option, Salzburg Airport serves as the primary gateway for international travelers. With regular flights from major European hubs such as London, Frankfurt, Amsterdam, and Vienna, operated by renowned carriers like Austrian Airlines, Lufthansa, and easyJet, reaching Salzburg by air is a breeze. The airport's proximity to the city center, a mere 4 kilometers away, further enhances its appeal, ensuring a swift and hassle-free transfer upon arrival.

- **Securing the Best Airfare Deals:**
  - **Advance Booking is Key**: Particularly during peak travel seasons, including the summer months and the Christmas holidays, airfares tend to escalate as the departure date approaches. Secure the most competitive rates by booking your flights well in advance.
  - **Embrace Flexibility**: If your travel dates are not set in stone, consider flying on weekdays or during off-peak hours to potentially unlock lower fares.
  - **Harness the Power of Comparison**: Leverage online flight comparison platforms like Skyscanner,

Kayak, or Google Flights to effortlessly juxtapose prices across various airlines and travel dates, ensuring you secure the most cost-effective option.

- **Stay Informed with Airline Newsletters**: Subscribe to email newsletters from your preferred airlines to receive timely updates on exclusive deals, promotions, and flash sales.

- **Explore Budget Airlines**: While traditional carriers offer comprehensive services, budget airlines like easyJet and Ryanair frequently present compelling fares, allowing you to allocate your travel budget more efficiently. However, remain cognizant of potential ancillary fees for baggage and other services.

By Rail

- **Salzburg Hauptbahnhof (Central Station)**: Salzburg's central train station stands as a vital transportation nexus, boasting excellent connectivity to cities across Austria, Germany, and other European countries. High-speed rail services like Railjet and ICE ensure a comfortable and efficient journey, seamlessly integrating Salzburg into the wider European rail network.

- **Optimizing Your Rail Travel Budget:**

- **Early Bird Catches the Worm**: Train ticket prices tend to increase as the travel date nears, so booking your tickets in advance is a prudent strategy to secure the best fares.

- **Explore Rail Passes**: If your itinerary includes extensive train travel within Austria or Europe, consider investing in a rail pass such as the Eurail Pass or Interrail Pass. These passes can offer substantial savings compared to purchasing individual tickets for each journey.

- **Stay Alert for Special Offers**: Train operators periodically introduce discounted fares for specific routes or travel periods. Monitor their websites or subscribe to their newsletters to stay abreast of these enticing promotions.

- **Travel Off-Peak**: Whenever possible, avoid traveling during peak times like rush hour or weekends, as fares tend to be higher during these periods. Opting for off-peak travel times can potentially lead to more affordable ticket options.

By Bus

- **Salzburg Bus Terminal**: Conveniently situated near the central train station, the bus terminal serves as a gateway for bus travel, offering connections to numerous destinations within Austria and neighboring countries. Reputable bus companies like FlixBus and Eurolines provide budget-conscious travelers with a practical and comfortable means of reaching Salzburg.

- **Maximizing Savings on Bus Travel:**

    o **Book Online and in Advance**: Bus tickets typically come at a lower cost when purchased online, especially during periods of high demand. Secure your seat early to avoid disappointment and potential price increases.

    o **Embrace Flexible Travel Times**: Early morning or late-night bus departures often present more economical options compared to those during peak hours. If your schedule allows, consider these off-peak travel times to potentially reduce your transportation expenses.

    o **Investigate Discounts**: Certain bus companies extend discounts to specific demographics such as students, seniors, or groups. Inquire about these potential savings when making your booking.

    o **Consider Overnight Buses**: If you're seeking to optimize your travel budget, overnight buses can present an attractive alternative, enabling you to save on accommodation costs while maximizing your time for exploration.

No matter your chosen mode of transport, reaching Salzburg is a journey in itself, setting the tone for the unforgettable experiences that await in this captivating city.

Visas and Entry Requirements

As you prepare for your Salzburg adventure, understanding the visa and entry requirements is crucial for a smooth and hassle-free journey. While specific regulations may vary depending on your nationality, here's a comprehensive overview to guide you:

Citizens of the European Union (EU), European Economic Area (EEA), and Switzerland:

- Visa-free entry: Enjoy the freedom of visa-free travel to Austria for stays up to 90 days within a 180-day period.

- Valid travel document: Carry a valid passport or national identity card that remains valid for at least three months beyond your intended stay.

- Sufficient funds: Demonstrate the ability to support yourself financially during your stay, typically around €75 per day.

- Health insurance: Possess comprehensive travel health insurance covering medical expenses and repatriation, with a minimum coverage of €30,000.

Citizens of Visa-Exempt Countries:

- Visa-free entry: Several countries, including the United States, Canada, Australia, New Zealand, and Japan, enjoy visa-free entry to Austria for stays up to 90 days within a 180-day period.

- ETIAS Authorization: From November 2023, citizens of visa-exempt countries will need to obtain an ETIAS (European Travel Information and Authorisation System) authorization before traveling to Austria. This can be done online and typically costs €7.

- Valid travel document: Similar to EU/EEA/Swiss citizens, carry a valid passport that remains valid for at least three months beyond your intended stay.

- Sufficient funds and health insurance: Ensure you have sufficient funds and comprehensive travel health insurance, as outlined above.

Citizens of Other Countries:

- Schengen Visa (Type C): If your country is not visa-exempt, you'll need to apply for a Schengen Visa (Type C) at the

Austrian embassy or consulate in your home country. This visa allows for stays up to 90 days within a 180-day period and is valid for travel within the entire Schengen Area.

- Required documents: Typically include a completed visa application form, a valid passport, passport-sized photos, proof of accommodation, travel itinerary, travel health insurance, and proof of sufficient funds.

- Processing time: Allow ample time for visa processing, which can take several weeks or even months, depending on your nationality and the embassy's workload.

- Additional requirements: Specific requirements may apply depending on your nationality and purpose of travel. Check with the Austrian embassy or consulate for detailed information.

Important Notes:

- ETIAS: Remember that from November 2023, even if you are visa-exempt, you will need an ETIAS authorization to enter Austria.

- Visa validity: Ensure your visa or ETIAS authorization covers the entire duration of your stay in Austria.

- Passport validity: Your passport must be valid for at least three months beyond your planned departure date from the Schengen Area.

- COVID-19 regulations: Stay updated on any COVID-19-related entry requirements or restrictions, as these may change depending on the pandemic situation.

By understanding and fulfilling the visa and entry requirements applicable to your nationality, you can ensure a seamless and stress-free journey to Salzburg. Remember to check the official website of the Austrian embassy or consulate in your home country for the most up-to-date and accurate information.

With your travel documents in order, you can focus on the exciting adventures that await you in Mozart's city.

Accommodation Options

Salzburg, with its blend of historic charm and modern amenities, offers a diverse range of accommodation options to suit every traveler's taste and budget. Whether you're seeking a luxurious retreat, a cozy guesthouse, or a budget-friendly hostel, you'll find the perfect place to rest your head after a day of exploring Mozart's city.

Areas to Consider for First-Time Visitors:

- **Altstadt (Old Town):** The heart of Salzburg, Altstadt is a UNESCO World Heritage Site brimming with historic landmarks, charming streets, and vibrant squares. Staying here puts you within walking distance of major attractions, restaurants, and shops, making it an ideal choice for first-time visitors. However, be prepared for slightly higher prices and potential noise levels in this popular area.

- **Neustadt (New Town):** Just across the Salzach River from Altstadt, Neustadt offers a quieter and more affordable alternative. It's still within easy walking distance of the main attractions, and its tree-lined streets and elegant buildings create a pleasant atmosphere.

- **Mönchsberg and Nonntal:** These hilly neighborhoods offer stunning views of the city and a more residential feel. While slightly farther from the center, they provide a peaceful retreat and easy access to scenic trails and outdoor activities.

- **Elisabeth-Vorstadt:** Located north of the city center, this district offers a mix of residential areas, shops, and restaurants. It's a good option for budget-conscious travelers and those seeking a more local experience.

Accommodation Recommendations:

Budget-Friendly:

- **YoHo International Youth Hostel:** This centrally located hostel offers clean and comfortable dorms and private rooms at affordable prices. It's a great option for solo travelers and backpackers seeking a social atmosphere.

- **Meininger Hotel Salzburg City Center:** This modern hotel offers a mix of dorms, private rooms, and family rooms, all with en-suite bathrooms. Its central location and amenities like a guest kitchen and laundry facilities make it a popular choice for budget-minded travelers.

- **Institut St. Sebastian:** This unique hostel, housed in a former monastery, offers basic but comfortable accommodations in a historic setting. It's a great option for those seeking a peaceful and spiritual atmosphere.

Mid-Range:

- **Hotel am Mirabellplatz:** This charming hotel offers comfortable rooms and a prime location just steps from Mirabell Palace and Gardens. Its friendly staff and delicious breakfast make it a popular choice for couples and families.

- **Hotel Goldgasse:** This boutique hotel, located in the heart of Altstadt, offers stylish rooms and a rooftop terrace with stunning city views. Its central location and personalized service make it an excellent choice for discerning travelers.

- **Altstadthotel Weisse Taube:** This historic hotel, housed in a 14th-century building, offers a blend of old-world charm and modern amenities. Its central location and cozy atmosphere make it a favorite among couples and solo travelers.

Luxury:

- **Hotel Sacher Salzburg:** This iconic hotel, overlooking the Salzach River, offers luxurious accommodations, impeccable service, and a Michelin-starred restaurant. It's the perfect choice for those seeking a truly indulgent experience.

- **Hotel Goldener Hirsch, a Luxury Collection Hotel:** This historic hotel, located in the heart of Altstadt, offers elegant rooms, a refined atmosphere, and a Michelin-starred restaurant. It's a favorite among discerning travelers seeking a blend of tradition and luxury.

- **Hotel Schloss Mönchstein:** This castle hotel, perched on a hill overlooking the city, offers breathtaking views, luxurious accommodations, and a tranquil atmosphere. It's an ideal choice for romantic getaways and special occasions.

Additional Tips for Choosing Accommodation:

- Consider your budget: Determine how much you're willing to spend on accommodation and choose an option that fits your financial constraints.

- Prioritize location: If you want to be in the heart of the action, choose a hotel in Altstadt or Neustadt. If you prefer a quieter atmosphere, consider staying in Mönchsberg or Nonntal.

- Read reviews: Check online reviews from other travelers to get a sense of the hotel's atmosphere, amenities, and service.

- Book in advance: Especially during peak season, it's essential to book your accommodation well in advance to secure your preferred choice.

By carefully considering your priorities and exploring the diverse options available, you're sure to find the perfect accommodation to enhance your Salzburg experience. Whether you're indulging in luxury or embracing budget-friendly options, your chosen haven will provide a comfortable and welcoming retreat after a day of exploring Mozart's magical city.

Packing Essentials

Packing strategically for your Salzburg adventure ensures you're well-equipped to embrace the city's diverse climate and engage in its array of activities. Here's a practical packing list to guide you:

Clothing:

- Layering is key: Salzburg's weather can be unpredictable, so pack versatile layers that can be easily adjusted to changing conditions.

- Comfortable walking shoes: You'll likely do a lot of walking in Salzburg, so prioritize comfortable shoes that provide good support.

- Weather-appropriate attire:
    - Spring/Autumn: Pack long-sleeved shirts, sweaters, a light jacket, and a waterproof raincoat. Consider bringing a scarf and gloves for cooler evenings.
    - Summer: Bring lightweight clothing like t-shirts, shorts, and skirts. Include a swimsuit if you plan on visiting lakes or swimming pools. A light jacket or cardigan is useful for cooler evenings.

- Winter: Pack warm layers like thermal underwear, fleece jackets, and a heavy coat. Don't forget a hat, scarf, and gloves to protect yourself from the cold. Waterproof boots are also essential for snowy conditions.

- Formal attire: If you plan on attending concerts, operas, or upscale restaurants, pack a dress or suit for special occasions.

Accessories:

- Sunglasses: Protect your eyes from the sun, especially during the summer months.

- Hat: A hat provides shade and protects your head from the sun's rays.

- Sunscreen: Apply sunscreen regularly, even on cloudy days, to protect your skin from harmful UV rays.

- Insect repellent: During the warmer months, insect repellent can be helpful for outdoor activities.

- Umbrella or raincoat: Be prepared for occasional rain showers, especially during the spring and autumn months.

- Backpack or day bag: A comfortable backpack or day bag is essential for carrying your essentials while exploring the city.

Electronics:

- Universal travel adapter: Austria uses Type F electrical outlets, so bring a universal adapter to ensure compatibility with your electronic devices.

- Camera: Capture your Salzburg memories with a camera, whether it's a DSLR, a mirrorless camera, or your smartphone.

- Phone charger: Keep your phone charged and ready for navigation, communication, and capturing photos.

- Portable power bank: A power bank is handy for charging your devices on the go, especially if you're out exploring all day.

Documents:

- Passport: Your passport is essential for international travel. Make sure it's valid for at least six months beyond your planned departure date.

- Visa or ETIAS authorization: If required, ensure you have the necessary visa or ETIAS authorization for entry into Austria.

- Travel insurance: Travel insurance provides peace of mind in case of unexpected events like medical emergencies or trip cancellations.

- Printed copies of important documents: It's a good idea to have printed copies of your passport, visa, travel insurance, and other essential documents in case of loss or theft.

Other Essentials:

- Medications: Pack any prescription medications you need, along with over-the-counter medications for common ailments like headaches or colds.
- Toiletries: Bring your usual toiletries, including toothbrush, toothpaste, shampoo, conditioner, soap, and any other personal care items you need.
- First-aid kit: A basic first-aid kit is always a good idea for minor injuries or ailments.
- Travel guidebook or map: A guidebook or map can help you navigate the city and discover its many attractions.
- Phrasebook or language app: If you don't speak German, a phrasebook or language app can help you communicate with locals.
- Reusable water bottle: Stay hydrated and reduce waste by bringing a reusable water bottle.

By packing thoughtfully and strategically, you'll be well-prepared to enjoy all that Salzburg has to offer. Remember, it's always better to pack light and leave room in your luggage for souvenirs and treasures you'll discover along the way.

42 | SALZBURG TRAVEL GUIDE 2025

CHAPTER 2

Salzburg's Must-See Landmarks

Hohensalzburg Fortress

Perched atop the Festungsberg hill, the Hohensalzburg Fortress reigns supreme as an enduring symbol of Salzburg's power and resilience. Its imposing silhouette against the backdrop of the Alps is a sight that evokes awe and wonder, beckoning visitors to step back in time and explore its storied halls.

A Tapestry of History:

The fortress's origins date back to 1077, when Archbishop Gebhard initiated its construction as a strategic stronghold to protect the city and its archbishops. Over the centuries, successive rulers expanded and fortified the complex, transforming it into one of Europe's largest and most well-preserved medieval fortresses.

Its formidable walls and bastions have witnessed centuries of history, from sieges and battles to lavish feasts and courtly intrigues. The fortress served as a refuge for the archbishops during times of unrest and a symbol of their authority and power.

Today, it stands as a testament to Salzburg's rich past and a window into its fascinating history.

Architectural Marvels:

As you approach the fortress, its sheer scale and architectural grandeur will leave you breathless. The fortress complex comprises a series of interconnected buildings, courtyards, and towers, each with its unique character and charm.

The Romanesque and Gothic styles dominate the fortress's architecture, with later additions reflecting Renaissance and Baroque influences. The imposing outer walls, fortified gates, and defensive towers create a sense of impenetrable strength, while the interior spaces reveal a surprising elegance and sophistication.

Highlights include the Golden Hall, a lavishly decorated banquet hall adorned with gold leaf and intricate wood carvings, and the Prince's Chambers, where the archbishops once resided in opulent surroundings. The fortress also houses several museums, showcasing its history, art collections, and military artifacts.

Panoramic Vistas:

One of the fortress's greatest allurements is the breathtaking panoramic views it offers of Salzburg and its surroundings. From the fortress's ramparts and terraces, you can gaze upon the city's rooftops, spires, and domes, the winding Salzach River, and the majestic Alps in the distance. It's a vista that captures the essence of Salzburg's beauty and will leave an indelible impression on your memory.

Tips for Visiting and Exploring:

- Take the funicular: The Festungsbahn funicular railway offers a convenient and scenic way to reach the fortress. The ride takes just a few minutes and offers stunning views of the city as you ascend.

- Allow ample time: Exploring the fortress can easily take several hours, so plan your visit accordingly. Allow time to wander through the courtyards, visit the museums, and soak in the panoramic views.

- Consider a guided tour: A guided tour can provide valuable insights into the fortress's history and architecture, enhancing your understanding and appreciation of this landmark.

- Wear comfortable shoes: The fortress involves a fair amount of walking, both uphill and on uneven terrain. Wear comfortable shoes that provide good support.

- Check the weather: The fortress is open year-round, but weather conditions can affect your experience. Dress appropriately for the season and be prepared for wind and rain, especially during the colder months.

- Bring your camera: The fortress offers countless photo opportunities, so make sure to bring your camera to capture its beauty and grandeur.

- Enjoy the views: Take your time to relax and soak in the panoramic vistas from the fortress's ramparts and terraces. It's a truly unforgettable experience.

The Hohensalzburg Fortress is a must-see landmark for any visitor to Salzburg. Its rich history, architectural splendor, and stunning views make it a truly unforgettable experience. Whether you're a history buff, an architecture enthusiast, or simply someone who appreciates beauty and grandeur, the fortress will leave a lasting impression on your heart and soul.

Salzburg Cathedral

Standing proudly in the heart of Salzburg's Old Town, the Salzburg Cathedral (Salzburger Dom) is a testament to the city's rich spiritual and artistic heritage. This magnificent Baroque masterpiece, with its soaring dome and twin towers, dominates the skyline and beckons visitors to step inside its hallowed halls.

A Beacon of Faith and Power:

The cathedral's history is intertwined with that of Salzburg itself. Founded in 774 by Saint Rupert, it has been rebuilt and expanded several times over the centuries, reflecting the changing architectural styles and ambitions of its patrons. The current structure, completed in 1628, is a masterpiece of early Baroque architecture, designed by the Italian architect Santino Solari.

The cathedral served as the seat of the powerful prince-archbishops who ruled Salzburg for centuries. Its grandeur and opulence were intended to showcase their authority and inspire awe in the faithful. Today, it remains the spiritual center of the Archdiocese of Salzburg and a place of pilgrimage for Catholics from around the world.

Exterior Splendor:

The cathedral's facade, crafted from Untersberg marble, is a symphony of Baroque elegance. Its symmetrical design, ornate sculptures, and towering columns create a sense of harmony and grandeur. Four monumental statues grace the facade: the apostles Peter and Paul, and Salzburg's patron saints, Rupert and Virgil.

The central dome, reaching a height of 79 meters (259 feet), is a masterpiece of engineering and artistry. Its copper cladding shimmers in the sunlight, while its interior is adorned with frescoes depicting scenes from the Bible.

The twin towers, flanking the facade, add to the cathedral's imposing presence. They house a collection of bells, including the "Salzburg Bull," one of the largest bells in Austria.

Interior Treasures:

Stepping inside the cathedral, you'll be enveloped in an atmosphere of serenity and awe. The vast interior, bathed in natural light filtering through stained-glass windows, is a testament to the Baroque love of drama and theatricality.

The high altar, a focal point of the cathedral, is a masterpiece of Baroque sculpture and gilding. It depicts the Assumption of the Virgin Mary, surrounded by angels and saints. The ornate pulpit, crafted from marble and wood, is another highlight, showcasing intricate carvings and religious motifs.

The cathedral also houses several chapels, each with its own unique character and artistic treasures. The Marienkapelle, or Lady Chapel, is particularly noteworthy, with its delicate stuccowork and frescoes by Donato Mascagni.

Don't miss the opportunity to visit the crypt, where the remains of Salzburg's archbishops are interred. The crypt's somber atmosphere and historic significance offer a glimpse into the city's past.

Tips for Visiting:

- Respectful attire: Dress modestly when visiting the cathedral, covering shoulders and knees.

- Quiet contemplation: Maintain a respectful silence while inside the cathedral, allowing others to enjoy its peaceful atmosphere.

- Photography: Photography is generally allowed, but be mindful of flash photography and avoid disrupting worship services.

- Guided tours: Consider joining a guided tour to gain deeper insights into the cathedral's history, architecture, and artistic treasures.

- Organ concerts: The cathedral hosts regular organ concerts, showcasing the magnificent Klais organ. Check the schedule for upcoming performances.

The Salzburg Cathedral is a must-see landmark for any visitor to Salzburg. Its grandeur, significance, and artistic treasures offer a glimpse into the city's rich spiritual and cultural heritage. Whether you're a devout Catholic, an architecture enthusiast, or simply someone who appreciates beauty and history, the cathedral will leave a lasting impression on your heart and soul.

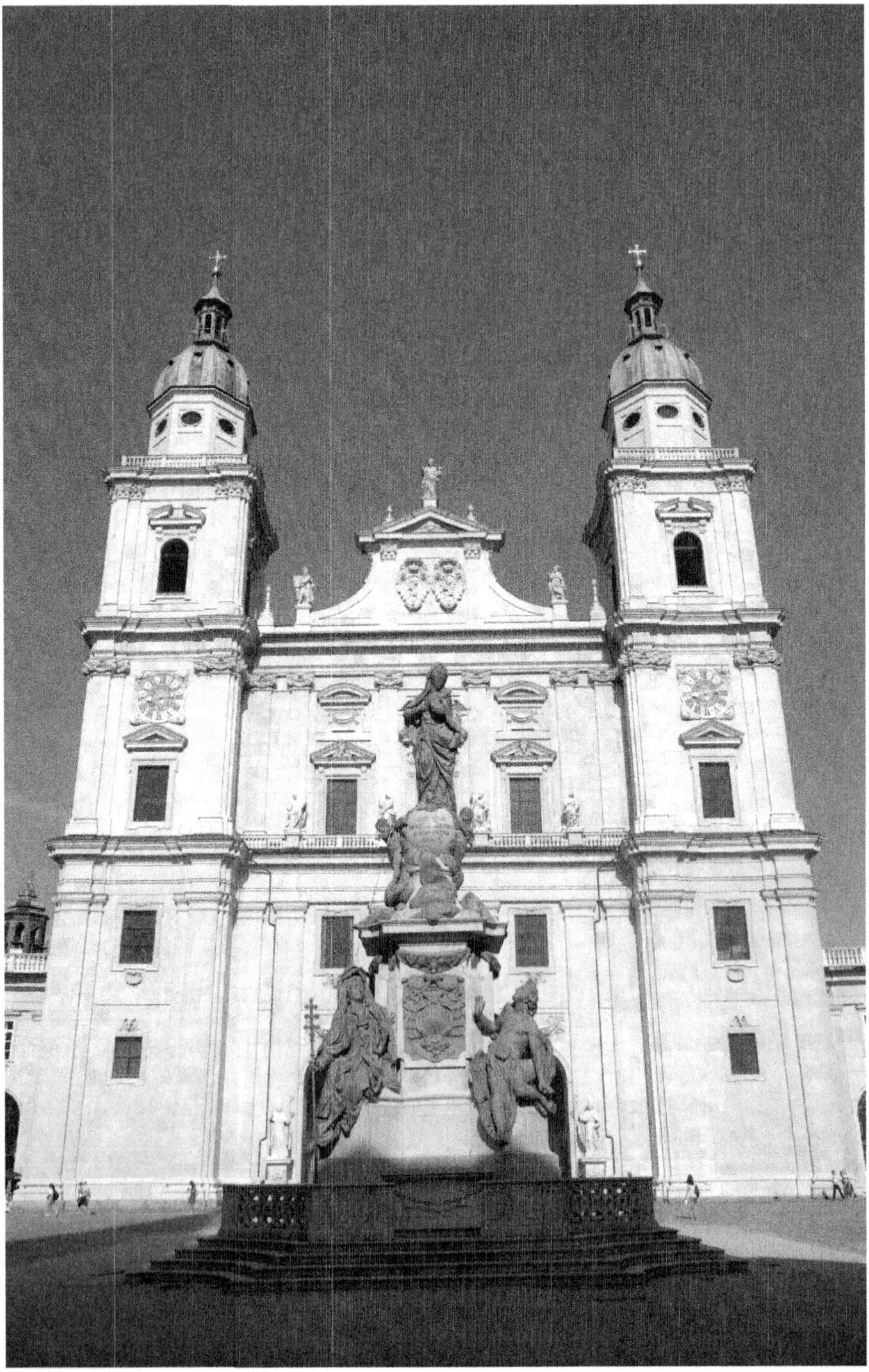

51 | SALZBURG TRAVEL GUIDE 2025

Mirabell Palace and Gardens

Nestled on the right bank of the Salzach River, Mirabell Palace and Gardens stand as a testament to Salzburg's Baroque splendor and enduring allure. This magnificent ensemble, with its graceful architecture, meticulously manicured gardens, and captivating views, is a feast for the senses and a haven of tranquility in the heart of the city.

A Palace Born of Love:

Mirabell Palace's story begins in 1606 when Prince-Archbishop Wolf Dietrich von Raitenau, smitten by his mistress Salome Alt, commissioned its construction as a testament to his love. Originally named Altenau Castle, it was later renamed Mirabell, meaning "admirable" and "beautiful" in Italian, reflecting its captivating elegance.

The palace has witnessed centuries of history, serving as a residence for the prince-archbishops and later as a governmental building. Today, it remains a symbol of Salzburg's rich past and a popular destination for visitors from around the world.

Architectural Grace:

Mirabell Palace's architecture is a harmonious blend of Baroque and Rococo styles, showcasing elaborate ornamentation, graceful curves, and a sense of lightness and airiness. The palace's facade, adorned with statues and decorative elements, exudes a sense of grandeur and sophistication.

The interior spaces are equally impressive, featuring ornate ceilings, gilded moldings, and exquisite frescoes. The Marble Hall, a masterpiece of Baroque design, is renowned for its acoustics and serves as a venue for concerts and events.

Gardens of Enchantment:

The palace's gardens are a masterpiece of landscaping, meticulously designed to create a sense of harmony and balance. Geometrically arranged flowerbeds, sculpted hedges, and ornate fountains create a visual symphony that delights the eye.

The Pegasus Fountain, with its winged horse statue, is a focal point of the gardens and a popular photo spot. The Dwarf Garden, featuring a collection of whimsical gnome statues, adds a touch of playfulness to the landscape.

The Sound of Music Connection:

Mirabell Gardens gained international fame as a filming location for the iconic movie "The Sound of Music." The Do-Re-Mi steps, where Maria and the von Trapp children sing their way through the musical scale, are a must-visit for fans of the film. The Pegasus Fountain and the rose garden also feature prominently in memorable scenes.

Exploring the Palace and Gardens:

- The Marble Hall: Admire the exquisite Baroque architecture and acoustics of this grand hall, where Mozart himself once performed.

- The gardens: Wander through the meticulously manicured gardens, discovering hidden corners and enjoying the serene atmosphere.

- The Pegasus Fountain: Take a photo with this iconic landmark, featured in "The Sound of Music."

- The Dwarf Garden: Delight in the whimsical charm of this collection of gnome statues.

- The Orangery: Visit this historic greenhouse, now used for concerts and events.

Tips for Visiting:

- Free admission: The gardens are open to the public free of charge, making it a budget-friendly attraction.

- Guided tours: Consider joining a guided tour to learn more about the palace's history and architecture.

- Concerts: Check the schedule for concerts and events held in the Marble Hall and Orangery.

- Photography: Capture the beauty of the palace and gardens with your camera, but be respectful of other visitors.

Mirabell Palace and Gardens are a must-see destination for any visitor to Salzburg. Its elegant architecture, enchanting gardens, and cinematic charm offer a truly unforgettable experience. Whether you're a fan of "The Sound of Music," a history buff, or simply someone who appreciates beauty and tranquility, Mirabell will leave a lasting impression on your heart and soul.

Mozart's Birthplace and Residence

Mozart's Birthplace, Salzburg

Salzburg's inextricable link to Wolfgang Amadeus Mozart, the prodigious composer whose melodies continue to enchant the world, is embodied in two significant landmarks: his birthplace and his residence. These historic sites offer a glimpse into the life and times of this musical maestro, allowing visitors to trace his footsteps and connect with his extraordinary legacy.

Mozart's Birthplace (Mozarts Geburtshaus):

- A Humble Beginning: Nestled on the bustling Getreidegasse, Mozart's birthplace stands as a testament to his humble beginnings. This yellow-hued townhouse, now a museum, was where Mozart was born on January

27, 1756, and spent his formative years. The museum meticulously preserves the ambiance of 18th-century Salzburg, showcasing original furnishings, musical instruments, and personal belongings that offer insights into the Mozart family's life.

- Stepping into Mozart's World: As you explore the museum, you'll encounter a treasure trove of artifacts that illuminate Mozart's early years. The third-floor apartment, where Mozart was born, has been faithfully restored, offering a glimpse into the domestic life of the Mozart family. Letters, portraits, and musical scores provide intimate details about Mozart's childhood, his relationship with his family, and his burgeoning musical talent.

- Practical Information for Visitors:
    - Location: Getreidegasse 9, Salzburg
    - Opening Hours: Daily, 9 am to 5:30 pm (extended hours in July and August)
    - Admission: Adults €12, Students €4.50, Children (6-14) €3.50, Family Ticket €24
    - Audio guides: Available in multiple languages to enhance your understanding of the exhibits.

- Allow at least 1-2 hours for your visit to fully appreciate the museum's offerings.

Mozart's Residence (Mozart-Wohnhaus):

- A New Chapter: In 1773, the Mozart family moved across the Salzach River to a more spacious residence on Makartplatz. This elegant townhouse, now known as Mozart's Residence, served as the family's home for over a decade. It was here that Mozart composed some of his most celebrated works, including symphonies, concertos, and operas.

- Echoes of Creativity: The museum within Mozart's Residence provides a fascinating glimpse into his creative process and personal life during this period. Original furnishings, musical instruments, and personal belongings paint a vivid picture of Mozart's daily life and artistic pursuits. The "Tanzmeisterhaus" annex, where Mozart composed and rehearsed, offers a unique opportunity to connect with his creative spirit.

- Practical Information for Visitors:
    - Location: Makartplatz 8, Salzburg
    - Opening Hours: Daily, 9 am to 5:30 pm (extended hours in July and August)

- Admission: Adults €12, Students €4.50, Children (6-14) €3.50, Family Ticket €24 (Combined ticket with Mozart's Birthplace available)
- Audio guides: Available in multiple languages.
- Allow at least 1-2 hours for your visit to fully explore the museum and its exhibits.

Beyond the Museums:

- Mozart's Legacy: Salzburg's connection to Mozart extends beyond these two museums. You'll find traces of his presence throughout the city, from statues and monuments to concert halls and festivals dedicated to his music. The annual Mozart Week and Salzburg Festival are prime examples of how Salzburg continues to celebrate and honor its most famous son.

- Immerse Yourself in Mozart's World: To truly experience Mozart's Salzburg, consider attending a concert or opera in one of the city's historic venues. The Salzburg Marionette Theatre offers charming puppet performances of Mozart's operas, while the Salzburg Mozarteum Foundation organizes a variety of concerts and events throughout the year.

Visiting Mozart's birthplace and residence is a pilgrimage for music lovers and a fascinating journey into the life of a genius. These historic sites offer a unique opportunity to connect with Mozart's legacy and gain a deeper appreciation for his extraordinary contributions to the world of music.

Getreidegasse

In the heart of Salzburg's Old Town lies a street that encapsulates the city's timeless charm: Getreidegasse. This narrow, cobblestone lane, lined with elegant Baroque buildings and adorned with wrought-iron guild signs, is a testament to Salzburg's rich history and vibrant culture. As you stroll through its picturesque passageways, you'll be transported to a bygone era, where traditional crafts and timeless elegance reign supreme.

A Shopper's Paradise:

Getreidegasse is renowned for its unique blend of traditional shops and international brands. Here, you'll find everything from exquisite jewelry and fine leather goods to artisanal chocolates and handmade souvenirs. The street's narrow width and elevated passageways create an intimate and inviting atmosphere, perfect for leisurely browsing and discovering hidden treasures.

The street's most famous address is undoubtedly number 9, the birthplace of Wolfgang Amadeus Mozart. This yellow-hued townhouse, now a museum, is a pilgrimage site for music lovers from around the world. Even if you don't plan on visiting the museum, take a moment to admire its facade and imagine the young Mozart taking his first steps into the world of music.

Beyond Mozart's Birthplace:

While Mozart's birthplace is undoubtedly a highlight, Getreidegasse offers much more to explore. The street's many passageways, known as "Durchhäuser," lead to charming courtyards and hidden shops. Take a detour down one of these alleyways to discover unique boutiques, cozy cafes, and historic landmarks.

The guild signs, hanging above the doorways, are a reminder of Salzburg's rich craft traditions. These intricate wrought-iron signs, often depicting the trade or profession of the shop's owner, add a touch of artistry and authenticity to the street.

Tips for Exploring:

- Take your time: Getreidegasse is best explored at a leisurely pace. Allow yourself plenty of time to browse the shops, admire the architecture, and soak in the atmosphere.

- Look up: Don't forget to look up at the buildings' facades and the intricate guild signs. You'll discover hidden details and artistic treasures.

- Explore the passageways: Venture down the Durchhäuser to discover hidden courtyards, shops, and historic landmarks.

- Visit Mozart's birthplace: If you're a music lover, don't miss the opportunity to visit Mozart's birthplace and museum.

- Enjoy a coffee or pastry: Stop at one of the many cafes along Getreidegasse for a coffee, pastry, or traditional Austrian treat.

- Shop for souvenirs: Getreidegasse offers a wide selection of souvenirs, from traditional crafts to Mozart-themed memorabilia.

Beyond Shopping:

Getreidegasse is more than just a shopping street. It's a living testament to Salzburg's history and culture. As you stroll through its charming lanes, you'll encounter street performers, musicians, and artists, adding to the vibrant atmosphere.

Take a break from shopping to admire the architecture, explore the passageways, and people-watch in one of the many squares.

Getreidegasse is a place to slow down, savor the moment, and immerse yourself in the heart and soul of Salzburg.

Whether you're a shopaholic, a history buff, or simply someone who appreciates beauty and charm, Getreidegasse is a must-visit destination in Salzburg. Its unique blend of traditional shops, historic landmarks, and vibrant atmosphere will leave a lasting impression on your memory.

63 | SALZBURG TRAVEL GUIDE 2025

64 | SALZBURG TRAVEL GUIDE 2025

CHAPTER 3

Salzburg's Hidden Gems

Mönchsberg

While Salzburg's Old Town captivates with its Baroque grandeur, a hidden gem awaits just a stone's throw away: Mönchsberg, a verdant hill that rises majestically above the city, offering a serene escape and breathtaking vistas. This natural oasis, crisscrossed by scenic trails and dotted with cultural landmarks, invites you to step off the beaten path and discover a different side of Salzburg.

A Natural Sanctuary:

Mönchsberg, meaning "Monk's Mountain," is a haven of tranquility amidst the bustling city. Its forested slopes, lush meadows, and winding paths provide a welcome respite from the crowds, offering a chance to reconnect with nature and soak in the serenity. As you wander through its trails, you'll encounter a diverse ecosystem, from ancient trees and wildflowers to playful squirrels and chirping birds.

The hill's strategic location, overlooking the Salzach River and the Old Town, has made it a place of significance throughout history.

Remnants of medieval fortifications and watchtowers dot its slopes, whispering tales of Salzburg's past. Today, Mönchsberg is a beloved recreational area, attracting locals and visitors alike seeking fresh air, exercise, and stunning views.

Scenic Trails and Panoramic Vistas:

Mönchsberg's network of trails caters to all levels of hikers, from leisurely strolls to challenging climbs. The Mönchsberg Lift, a modern funicular, offers a convenient way to ascend the hill, while those seeking a more active experience can hike up from the Old Town.

As you ascend, you'll be rewarded with increasingly spectacular views of Salzburg's skyline. The iconic Hohensalzburg Fortress dominates the panorama, while the city's spires, domes, and rooftops spread out like a tapestry below. The Salzach River winds its way through the landscape, reflecting the sunlight and adding a touch of sparkle to the scene.

On a clear day, you can even glimpse the snow-capped peaks of the Alps in the distance, creating a truly breathtaking vista.

Cultural Delights:

Mönchsberg is not only a natural haven but also a cultural hub. The Museum der Moderne, perched on the hill's edge, showcases contemporary art from around the world. Its sleek, minimalist architecture contrasts beautifully with the surrounding landscape, while its collection challenges and inspires visitors.

The Museum's rooftop terrace offers another vantage point for admiring the city views, while its café provides a welcome respite for refreshments and contemplation.

Other cultural landmarks on Mönchsberg include the Richterhöhe viewpoint, offering unobstructed views of the Hohensalzburg Fortress, and the Bürgerwehr, a historic shooting range with a charming beer garden.

Tips for Exploring:

- Take the Mönchsberg Lift: For a convenient and scenic ascent, take the Mönchsberg Lift from the Old Town.

- Hike up: If you're feeling energetic, hike up one of the many trails leading to the top.

- Visit the Museum der Moderne: Immerse yourself in contemporary art and enjoy the museum's stunning views.

- Relax at the M32 café: Take a break at the Museum der Moderne's café for refreshments and panoramic vistas.

- Explore the trails: Wander through Mönchsberg's network of trails, discovering hidden corners and enjoying the natural beauty.

- Pack a picnic: Enjoy a leisurely picnic lunch amidst the scenic surroundings.

- Watch the sunset: Witness a spectacular sunset over Salzburg from one of Mönchsberg's viewpoints.

Mönchsberg is a hidden gem that offers a unique perspective on Salzburg. Its scenic trails, captivating views, and cultural landmarks create a truly enriching experience. Whether you're seeking tranquility, outdoor adventure, or artistic inspiration, Mönchsberg will leave a lasting impression on your heart and soul.

Hellbrunn Palace and Trick Fountains

Just a short journey south of Salzburg's bustling center, Hellbrunn Palace and its enchanting trick fountains offer a delightful escape into a world of whimsy and surprise. This Renaissance gem, nestled amidst lush greenery, invites you to embrace the playful spirit of its creator, Prince-Archbishop Markus Sittikus von Hohenems, and experience a unique blend of history, artistry, and mischievous fun.

A Palace of Pleasure:

Built between 1613 and 1619, Hellbrunn Palace was conceived as a summer retreat for the prince-archbishop and his guests. Its architecture, a harmonious blend of Italian and German Renaissance styles, reflects the era's love of beauty, symmetry, and grandeur. The palace's elegant facade, adorned with statues and frescoes, sets the stage for the playful surprises that await within its walls and gardens.

The Trick Fountains: A Symphony of Water and Wit

The true highlight of Hellbrunn is its ingenious trick fountains, a testament to the prince-archbishop's mischievous sense of humor and love of spectacle. These hydraulic marvels, concealed throughout the gardens, are designed to surprise and delight unsuspecting visitors with unexpected sprays of water.

As you wander through the manicured grounds, you'll encounter a series of playful water features, from hidden jets that spring to life from seemingly innocent statues to elaborate table settings that drench unsuspecting diners. The Mechanical Theatre, a water-powered marvel, features miniature figures enacting scenes from daily life, all set to the music of a water-driven organ.

The trick fountains are not just a source of amusement; they also represent a remarkable feat of engineering for their time. The intricate system of pipes, valves, and reservoirs, powered entirely by natural water pressure, is a testament to the ingenuity and creativity of the Renaissance era.

Beyond the Fountains:

While the trick fountains are the main attraction, Hellbrunn offers much more to explore. The palace's interior, adorned with frescoes and stuccowork, provides a glimpse into the opulent lifestyle of the prince-archbishops. The Stone Theater, an open-air amphitheater carved into the hillside, is a unique venue for concerts and performances.

The surrounding parkland, with its manicured lawns, wooded trails, and scenic ponds, offers a peaceful retreat for nature lovers. The Hellbrunn Zoo, home to a variety of animals from around the world, is a popular destination for families.

Tips for Visiting:

- Guided tour: A guided tour of the trick fountains is highly recommended. The knowledgeable guides will reveal the secrets behind the waterworks and share entertaining anecdotes about their history.

- Dress appropriately: Be prepared to get wet! Wear comfortable shoes and clothing that you don't mind getting splashed.

- Explore the grounds: Allow ample time to wander through the palace gardens and discover hidden fountains and scenic spots.

- Visit the Stone Theater: Check the schedule for concerts and performances in this unique outdoor venue.

- Bring your camera: Capture the playful moments and unexpected surprises with your camera.

Hellbrunn Palace and its trick fountains are a must-see destination for any visitor to Salzburg. Its whimsical charm, historical significance, and playful atmosphere create a truly unique and memorable experience. Whether you're young or young at heart, Hellbrunn will leave you with a smile on your face and a sense of wonder in your heart.

St. Peter's Abbey and Cemetery

Nestled in the heart of Salzburg's Old Town, St. Peter's Abbey (Stift Sankt Peter) is a testament to the city's enduring spiritual heritage and a haven of tranquility amidst the bustling urban landscape. This Benedictine monastery, founded in 696 by Saint Rupert, is considered one of the oldest continuously inhabited monasteries in the German-speaking world. Its rich history, architectural splendor, and picturesque cemetery offer a unique glimpse into Salzburg's past and a serene escape from the modern world.

A Living Legacy:

St. Peter's Abbey has played a pivotal role in Salzburg's development for over a millennium. It served as a center of learning and culture during the Middle Ages, attracting scholars and artists from across Europe. Its monks contributed significantly to the city's intellectual and spiritual life, establishing schools, libraries, and hospitals.

The abbey's architectural evolution reflects its long and storied history. The current church, rebuilt in the 12th century, showcases a harmonious blend of Romanesque, Gothic, and Baroque elements. Its interior, adorned with ornate stuccowork, frescoes, and gilded altars, is a testament to the Baroque love of drama and theatricality.

The abbey's library, one of the oldest in Austria, houses a treasure trove of manuscripts, incunabula, and rare books. Its collection spans centuries of human knowledge and creativity, offering a window into the intellectual pursuits of generations past.

A Cemetery of Serenity:

Adjacent to the abbey lies St. Peter's Cemetery (Petersfriedhof), a picturesque burial ground that exudes a sense of peace and contemplation. Its origins date back to Roman times, making it one of the oldest cemeteries in Europe.

The cemetery's winding paths, shaded by ancient trees, lead to a collection of ornate tombs, crypts, and chapels. Many notable figures, including Mozart's sister Nannerl and the composer Michael Haydn, are interred here, their final resting places adorned with poignant epitaphs and sculptures.

The catacombs, carved into the Mönchsberg cliff face, offer a fascinating glimpse into early Christian burial practices. These dimly lit chambers, once used for religious gatherings and hermitage, now house the remains of Salzburg's early Christians.

Exploring St. Peter's:

- The Abbey Church: Admire the architectural beauty and artistic treasures of this historic church.

- The library: If you have a special interest, inquire about access to the abbey's library and its collection of rare books and manuscripts.

- The cemetery: Wander through the peaceful cemetery, discovering its ornate tombs and historical significance.

- The catacombs: Venture into the dimly lit catacombs for a glimpse into early Christian burial practices.

- The restaurant: Enjoy a traditional Austrian meal at the Stiftskeller St. Peter, one of the oldest restaurants in Europe.

Tips for Visiting:

- Respectful attire: Dress modestly when visiting the abbey and cemetery.

- Quiet contemplation: Maintain a respectful silence while exploring these sacred spaces.

- Photography: Photography is generally allowed, but be mindful of flash photography and avoid disrupting worship services.

- Guided tours: Consider joining a guided tour to learn more about the abbey's history, architecture, and artistic treasures.

- Mozart Dinner Concerts: Experience a unique evening of music and cuisine at the Mozart Dinner Concerts held in the abbey's Baroque Hall.

St. Peter's Abbey and Cemetery offer a unique blend of history, spirituality, and natural beauty. Whether you're seeking a moment of quiet reflection, a glimpse into Salzburg's past, or simply a peaceful escape from the city's hustle and bustle, this hidden gem will leave a lasting impression on your heart and soul.

Salzburg Museum

Nestled within the elegant walls of the Neue Residenz, the Salzburg Museum stands as a gateway to the city's rich and multifaceted history. This comprehensive museum invites visitors on a captivating journey through time, showcasing a vast collection of artifacts, artworks, and interactive exhibits that illuminate Salzburg's cultural heritage and illuminate its evolution from a Roman settlement to a modern European city.

A Treasure Trove of History and Culture:

The Salzburg Museum's collection spans a remarkable breadth, encompassing archaeology, art, and cultural history. As you wander through its galleries, you'll encounter a fascinating array of objects that tell the story of Salzburg's past, from prehistoric tools and Roman artifacts to medieval manuscripts and Baroque masterpieces.

The museum's permanent exhibitions provide a comprehensive overview of Salzburg's history, tracing its development from its early Celtic and Roman roots to its golden age as a Baroque principality. You'll learn about the city's salt trade, its religious and political institutions, and its vibrant artistic and cultural scene.

Highlights of the collection include:

- Archaeological treasures: Discover ancient tools, weapons, and everyday objects that offer insights into the lives of Salzburg's earliest inhabitants.

- Medieval art and manuscripts: Marvel at illuminated manuscripts, religious sculptures, and liturgical objects that reflect the city's spiritual heritage.

- Baroque masterpieces: Admire paintings, sculptures, and decorative arts from Salzburg's golden age, showcasing the opulence and grandeur of the Baroque era.

- Mozart memorabilia: Explore a collection of objects related to Salzburg's most famous son, including musical instruments, letters, and personal belongings.

- Folk art and traditions: Gain insights into the customs and traditions of Salzburg's rural communities through a collection of folk costumes, furniture, and handicrafts.

Beyond the Exhibits:

The Salzburg Museum offers more than just a static display of objects. Interactive exhibits, multimedia presentations, and educational programs engage visitors of all ages, bringing Salzburg's history to life in a dynamic and accessible way.

The museum also hosts temporary exhibitions throughout the year, showcasing specific aspects of Salzburg's cultural heritage or exploring contemporary artistic themes. These exhibitions offer a fresh perspective on the city's past and present, enriching the visitor experience.

Tips for Visiting:

- Allow ample time: The Salzburg Museum's vast collection requires at least 2-3 hours to explore thoroughly.
- Audio guides: Enhance your understanding of the exhibits with audio guides available in multiple languages.
- Special exhibitions: Check the museum's website for information on current and upcoming temporary exhibitions.

- Family-friendly activities: The museum offers interactive programs and workshops designed for children and families.

- Café and shop: Take a break at the museum's café or browse the shop for unique souvenirs and gifts.

The Salzburg Museum is a must-visit destination for anyone seeking to delve deeper into the city's rich history and cultural heritage. Its comprehensive collection, engaging exhibits, and educational programs offer a fascinating glimpse into the past, present, and future of this remarkable city. Whether you're a history buff, an art lover, or simply curious about Salzburg's story, the museum will leave you with a deeper appreciation for its unique charm and enduring legacy.

Residenzplatz and the Salzburg Residenz

At the very heart of Salzburg's Old Town lies Residenzplatz, a grand square that embodies the city's historical significance and architectural splendor. This expansive space, framed by majestic Baroque buildings and adorned with an iconic fountain, is a testament to Salzburg's past as a powerful ecclesiastical principality and a vibrant cultural hub. Dominating one side of the square stands the Salzburg Residenz, the former palace of the prince-archbishops, a testament to their wealth, influence, and artistic patronage.

Residenzplatz: A Stage for History and Festivities

Residenzplatz has been the epicenter of Salzburg's social and political life for centuries. Its vast expanse has witnessed countless historical events, from grand processions and coronations to public executions and celebrations. Today, it remains a vibrant gathering place, hosting markets, festivals, and concerts throughout the year.

The square's focal point is the Residenzbrunnen, a magnificent Baroque fountain sculpted by Tommaso di Garona in 1661. Its central figure, Atlas, supports the globe on his shoulders, symbolizing the prince-archbishops' worldly power and divine authority. The surrounding figures represent the four rivers of Salzburg: the Salzach, the Inn, the Traun, and the Enns.

The buildings that frame Residenzplatz showcase a harmonious blend of architectural styles, reflecting the city's evolution over time. The Salzburg Cathedral, with its imposing dome and twin towers, dominates the eastern side of the square. The Glockenspiel, a 35-bell carillon housed in the New Residenz, chimes daily, enchanting visitors with its melodies.

Salzburg Residenz: A Palace of Opulence

The Salzburg Residenz, a sprawling complex of buildings on the western side of Residenzplatz, served as the official residence of the prince-archbishops for over 500 years. Its construction began in the 12th century, with subsequent additions and renovations reflecting the changing tastes and ambitions of its occupants.

The palace's interior is a treasure trove of Baroque and Rococo artistry, showcasing lavishly decorated state rooms, grand staircases, and exquisite frescoes. The State Rooms, open to the public, offer a glimpse into the opulent lifestyle of the prince-archbishops, with their gilded ceilings, silk wall coverings, and priceless furniture.

The Residenz Gallery, housed within the palace, displays a collection of European paintings from the 16th to the 19th centuries, including works by Rembrandt, Rubens, and Brueghel. The Gallery's collection reflects the prince-archbishops' passion for art and their desire to showcase their wealth and cultural sophistication.

Historical Significance:

Residenzplatz and the Salzburg Residenz are not merely architectural landmarks; they are living testaments to Salzburg's rich history and cultural heritage. They embody the power and influence of the prince-archbishops, who shaped the city's destiny for centuries. They also reflect the artistic and cultural flourishing of the Baroque era, a period of unparalleled creativity and innovation.

Exploring the Square and Palace:

- Admire the Residenzbrunnen: Take a moment to appreciate the artistry and symbolism of this magnificent fountain.

- Visit the Salzburg Residenz: Explore the palace's State Rooms and the Residenz Gallery, immersing yourself in Baroque splendor and artistic treasures.

- Listen to the Glockenspiel: Enjoy the enchanting melodies of the Glockenspiel, which chimes daily at 7 am, 11 am, and 6 pm.

- Attend a concert or event: Check the schedule for concerts, operas, and other events held in the Residenzplatz or the palace's halls.

- People-watch: Relax on a bench and observe the vibrant activity in this central square, a microcosm of Salzburg's life.

Residenzplatz and the Salzburg Residenz offer a captivating glimpse into Salzburg's past and present. Their grandeur, historical significance, and artistic treasures create a truly enriching experience. Whether you're a history buff, an art lover, or simply someone who appreciates beauty and culture, these landmarks will leave a lasting impression on your heart and soul.

83 | SALZBURG TRAVEL GUIDE 2025

CHAPTER 4

Experiencing Salzburg's Culture

Salzburg Festival

The Salzburg Festival, held annually from late July to late August, is a cultural extravaganza that attracts artists and audiences from around the globe. This prestigious event, renowned for its exceptional quality and diverse programming, showcases the best of opera, theater, and classical music, transforming Salzburg into a vibrant hub of artistic expression.

A Legacy of Excellence:

Founded in 1920, the Salzburg Festival has a long and illustrious history. Its origins can be traced back to the efforts of Max Reinhardt, a renowned theater director, Hugo von Hofmannsthal, a poet and playwright, and Richard Strauss, a celebrated composer. Their vision was to create a festival that would showcase the finest artistic talents in a setting of unparalleled beauty and cultural significance.

Over the years, the festival has hosted some of the most celebrated artists of the 20th and 21st centuries, including

Herbert von Karajan, Leonard Bernstein, Maria Callas, and Plácido Domingo. Its commitment to artistic excellence and innovation has earned it a reputation as one of the world's premier cultural events.

A Diverse Program:

The Salzburg Festival's program is a feast for the senses, offering a wide range of performances to suit all tastes. Opera lovers can revel in productions of Mozart's masterpieces, as well as works by other renowned composers. Theater enthusiasts can enjoy classic plays and contemporary productions, while classical music aficionados can attend concerts featuring world-class orchestras, soloists, and ensembles.

In addition to the main program, the festival also offers a variety of fringe events, including chamber music concerts, recitals, and lectures. These events provide a more intimate and accessible way to experience the festival's artistic vibrancy.

Tips for Attending:

- Plan ahead: Tickets for the Salzburg Festival are in high demand, especially for popular performances. Book your tickets well in advance, especially if you're traveling during peak season.

- Consider a package: Several tour operators offer packages that include tickets to festival performances, accommodation, and other benefits. These packages can be a convenient and cost-effective way to experience the festival.

- Explore different venues: The festival takes place in various venues throughout Salzburg, each with its unique atmosphere and charm. Consider attending performances in different locations to experience the full range of the festival's offerings.

- Attend a dress rehearsal: If you're on a budget, consider attending a dress rehearsal. These performances offer a glimpse into the creative process and are often available at a fraction of the price of regular tickets.

- Embrace the atmosphere: The Salzburg Festival is more than just a series of performances. It's a celebration of culture and creativity that permeates the entire city. Take time to soak in the atmosphere, attend fringe events, and mingle with fellow festival-goers.

Securing Tickets:

- Online: The official Salzburg Festival website is the most reliable source for purchasing tickets. You can browse the

- program, select your desired performances, and purchase tickets securely online.

- Box office: Tickets can also be purchased in person at the festival's box office, located in the Haus für Mozart.

- Authorized resellers: Be cautious when purchasing tickets from third-party resellers. Only purchase from authorized vendors to avoid scams and inflated prices.

- Last-minute options: If you're unable to secure tickets in advance, check the festival's website or box office for last-minute availability. Occasionally, tickets become available due to cancellations or changes in the program.

The Salzburg Festival is a cultural pilgrimage for music and art lovers, offering a unique opportunity to experience the finest artistic talents in a setting of unparalleled beauty and historical significance. Whether you're a seasoned festival-goer or a first-time visitor, the Salzburg Festival will leave you with unforgettable memories and a renewed appreciation for the power of artistic expression.

Additional Tips:

- Dress code: While there is no strict dress code for most performances, it's generally advisable to dress smartly.

- Arrive early: Allow ample time to reach the venue and find your seat, especially for popular performances.

- Enjoy the intermissions: Intermissions are a great opportunity to mingle with fellow festival-goers, enjoy refreshments, and soak in the atmosphere.

- Respect the performers: Please refrain from using electronic devices or taking photos during the performances.

With careful planning and a bit of flexibility, you can experience the magic of the Salzburg Festival and create memories that will last a lifetime.

Mozart Week

As the crisp winter air descends upon Salzburg, the city comes alive with the harmonious melodies of Mozart Week, an annual festival that celebrates the life and legacy of its most famous son. This prestigious event, held in late January and early February, attracts music lovers from around the globe, offering a diverse program of concerts, operas, chamber music, and lectures that pay homage to Mozart's genius.

A Symphony of Celebration:

Mozart Week, organized by the Mozarteum Foundation Salzburg, has been a beloved tradition since 1956. It serves as a platform for showcasing Mozart's vast oeuvre, performed by world-renowned artists in the very city where his musical journey began. The festival's program is carefully curated to offer a balanced mix of familiar favorites and lesser-known gems, providing both seasoned Mozart enthusiasts and newcomers with an enriching experience.

Concerts and Performances:

The heart of Mozart Week lies in its exceptional concerts and performances. World-class orchestras, soloists, and ensembles grace the stages of Salzburg's historic venues, including the Mozarteum's Great Hall, the Felsenreitschule, and the Salzburg Cathedral. The festival's program features a wide range of Mozart's works, from symphonies and concertos to operas and chamber music.

In addition to Mozart's compositions, the festival also explores the music of his contemporaries and influences, offering a broader perspective on the musical landscape of the 18th century. Guest artists often include renowned conductors, singers, and instrumentalists, ensuring a captivating and inspiring experience for audiences.

Beyond the Concerts:

Mozart Week is more than just a series of concerts. It's a celebration of Mozart's life and legacy, offering a variety of events and activities that delve deeper into his world. Lectures, workshops, and masterclasses provide insights into his creative process, his musical influences, and his impact on the world of music.

Exhibitions and guided tours explore Mozart's connection to Salzburg, showcasing his birthplace, his residence, and other significant landmarks. Special events, such as the Mozart Birthday Concert and the Mozart Matinee, add a festive touch to the festival.

Tips for Attending:

- Book early: Tickets for Mozart Week events, especially popular concerts and operas, sell out quickly. Plan your visit well in advance and secure your tickets as soon as possible.

- Explore the program: The festival's website offers a detailed program listing all events and performances. Take time to browse the offerings and choose the ones that appeal to you most.

- Consider a package: Several tour operators offer packages that include tickets to Mozart Week events, accommodation, and other benefits. These packages can be a convenient and cost-effective way to experience the festival.

- Attend a lecture or workshop: These events offer a deeper understanding of Mozart's music and his place in history.

- Explore Mozart's Salzburg: Take advantage of the festival's guided tours and exhibitions to explore Mozart's connection to the city.

Mozart Week is a must-attend event for any music lover visiting Salzburg. Its exceptional performances, insightful lectures, and festive atmosphere create a truly immersive experience that celebrates the genius of Mozart and his enduring legacy. Whether you're a seasoned Mozart aficionado or simply curious about his music, Mozart Week will leave you with a deeper appreciation for his artistry and a renewed sense of wonder at his extraordinary talent.

Salzburg Marionette Theatre

In the heart of Salzburg, a world of enchantment awaits at the Salzburg Marionette Theatre. This venerable institution, founded in 1913, has been captivating audiences for over a century with its exquisite puppetry and masterful performances of classic operas, plays, and fairy tales. Prepare to be transported to a realm where artistry and imagination intertwine, where wooden figures come alive with astonishing grace and emotion.

A Legacy of Artistry:

The Salzburg Marionette Theatre is a testament to the enduring power of puppetry, a centuries-old art form that transcends language and cultural barriers. Its founder, Professor Anton Aicher, envisioned a theater where puppets would not merely entertain but also inspire and educate. His vision has been carried forward by generations of puppeteers who have honed their craft to perfection, creating performances that are both visually stunning and emotionally resonant.

The theater's repertoire spans a wide range of genres, from Mozart's operas and Shakespeare's plays to beloved fairy tales and original productions. The puppets, meticulously crafted with attention to detail, become vessels for the puppeteers' artistry, their movements conveying a range of emotions that belie their inanimate forms.

A Feast for the Senses:

Attending a performance at the Salzburg Marionette Theatre is a multi-sensory experience. The elaborate stage sets, meticulously designed costumes, and expertly orchestrated lighting create a captivating visual spectacle. The puppets, manipulated with astonishing skill, seem to breathe and move with a life of their own. And the music, whether performed live or recorded, adds another layer of depth and emotion to the performance.

The theater's intimate setting, with its plush velvet seats and ornate decor, enhances the sense of magic and wonder. As the lights dim and the curtains rise, you'll be transported to a world where anything is possible, where puppets become heroes, villains, and lovers, and where timeless stories unfold before your very eyes.

Must-See Performances:

- Mozart's Operas: The Salzburg Marionette Theatre is renowned for its exquisite productions of Mozart's operas, including "The Magic Flute," "Don Giovanni," and "The Marriage of Figaro." These performances, faithful to the original scores and libretti, showcase the puppets' remarkable ability to convey the nuances of human emotion and the power of Mozart's music.

- Classic Plays: The theater also offers captivating renditions of classic plays by Shakespeare, Goethe, and other renowned playwrights. These productions, adapted for the puppet stage, retain the essence of the original works while adding a touch of whimsy and charm.

- Fairy Tales: For families and children, the theater presents enchanting performances of beloved fairy tales like "Cinderella," "Sleeping Beauty," and "Hansel and Gretel." These productions, filled with colorful characters and imaginative storytelling, are sure to delight audiences of all ages.

Tips for Attending:

- Book in advance: The Salzburg Marionette Theatre is a popular attraction, especially during peak season. Book your tickets well in advance to secure your preferred performance.

- Choose the right performance: The theater offers a variety of performances to suit different interests and age groups. Consider the length, genre, and language of the performance when making your selection.

- Arrive early: Allow ample time to reach the theater and find your seat, especially for popular performances.

- Immerse yourself in the experience: Let go of your preconceptions about puppetry and allow yourself to be enchanted by the artistry and magic of the performance.

The Salzburg Marionette Theatre is a cultural treasure that offers a unique and unforgettable experience. Its masterful puppetry, captivating performances, and enchanting atmosphere will leave a lasting impression on your heart and soul. Whether you're a seasoned theater-goer or a first-time visitor, the Salzburg

Marionette Theatre is a must-see destination that will transport you to a world of wonder and imagination.

Local Markets and Festivals

Beyond its grand concert halls and historic landmarks, Salzburg's vibrant culture truly comes alive in its bustling markets and festive celebrations. These gatherings, steeped in tradition and brimming with local flavor, offer a unique opportunity to connect with the city's soul, experience its authentic charm, and savor its culinary delights.

A Kaleidoscope of Colors and Flavors:

Salzburg's markets are a feast for the senses, showcasing a colorful array of local produce, handcrafted goods, and culinary specialties. Whether you're seeking fresh flowers, artisanal cheeses, or unique souvenirs, you'll find a treasure trove of delights waiting to be discovered.

- Grünmarkt: Nestled in the shadow of the majestic Universitätskirche (University Church), the Grünmarkt is a daily market that offers a vibrant glimpse into Salzburg's culinary scene. Stroll through its stalls and you'll find an abundance of fresh fruits and vegetables, fragrant herbs, and local specialties like Bauernbrot (farmer's bread) and Speck (cured ham).

- Schrannenmarkt: Held every Thursday morning in front of St. Andrew's Church, the Schrannenmarkt is a beloved tradition that dates back centuries. Here, local farmers and artisans gather to offer their wares, from organic produce and homemade jams to handcrafted ceramics and woven baskets.

- Rupertikirtag: This annual fair, held in late September, is a celebration of Salzburg's patron saint, Saint Rupert. The streets around the cathedral come alive with stalls selling traditional crafts, food, and drinks. It's a lively and festive occasion, offering a glimpse into Salzburg's rich cultural heritage.

- Christmas Markets: During the Advent season, Salzburg transforms into a winter wonderland, with charming Christmas markets popping up throughout the city. The largest and most famous is the Christkindlmarkt on Residenzplatz, where you'll find handcrafted ornaments, festive treats, and warming drinks like Glühwein (mulled wine).

Beyond the Markets:

Salzburg's calendar is filled with a variety of festivals and events throughout the year, each offering a unique glimpse into the city's cultural tapestry. From traditional folk celebrations to contemporary art exhibitions, there's always something happening in Salzburg.

- Salzburg Festival: This world-renowned festival, held in July and August, showcases the best of opera, theater, and classical music.

- Mozart Week: This annual festival, held in late January and early February, celebrates the life and legacy of Salzburg's most famous son, Wolfgang Amadeus Mozart.

- Easter Festival: This prestigious classical music festival takes place during Holy Week, offering a unique cultural experience.

- Sommer Szene Salzburg: This contemporary arts festival, held in July, features a diverse program of theater, dance, and performance art.

Tips for Experiencing Salzburg's Markets and Festivals:

- Embrace the atmosphere: Immerse yourself in the lively ambiance of Salzburg's markets and festivals, enjoying the sights, sounds, and flavors.

- Support local vendors: Purchase souvenirs, crafts, and food from local artisans and producers, contributing to the local economy and experiencing authentic Salzburg.

- Try the local specialties: Sample the delicious treats and culinary delights on offer, from freshly baked pastries to hearty Austrian dishes.

- Check the calendar: Consult the Salzburg tourism website or local event listings for up-to-date information on upcoming markets and festivals.

- Plan your visit: Some festivals, like the Salzburg Festival, require advance ticket purchases. Plan your visit accordingly to ensure you don't miss out on the events that interest you most.

Salzburg's markets and festivals offer a vibrant and authentic experience that complements the city's more formal cultural offerings. By exploring these lively gatherings, you'll gain a deeper appreciation for Salzburg's rich traditions, its creative spirit, and its warm hospitality.

Traditional Austrian Cuisine

Salzburg's culinary scene is a delightful tapestry of hearty flavors, rich traditions, and regional specialties. Influenced by both Austrian and Bavarian cuisines, Salzburg offers a diverse array of dishes that will tantalize your taste buds and leave you craving more. From savory classics to sweet indulgences, let's embark on a gastronomic journey through the heart of Salzburg's culinary landscape.

Must-Try Dishes:

- **Salzburger Nockerl:** This iconic dessert, unique to Salzburg, is a fluffy soufflé-like creation that resembles the snow-capped peaks of the surrounding mountains. Made with egg yolks, sugar, flour, and vanilla, it's baked until golden brown and served with a dusting of powdered sugar and a dollop of cranberry sauce. Its delicate texture and sweet flavor make it a must-try for any visitor.

- **Wiener Schnitzel:** This quintessential Austrian dish features a thin, breaded, and pan-fried veal cutlet. Traditionally served with a lemon wedge and a side of potato salad or parsley potatoes, it's a satisfying and flavorful meal that exemplifies Austrian comfort food.

- **Tafelspitz:** This boiled beef dish, often considered Austria's national dish, is a testament to the country's love of simple yet flavorful cuisine. The tender beef is simmered in a flavorful broth with root vegetables and spices, then served with a variety of accompaniments, such as horseradish sauce, apple horseradish, and chives sauce.

- **Kasnocken:** These cheesy dumplings, a specialty of the Salzburg region, are a hearty and comforting dish perfect for a cold winter day. Made with flour, eggs, cheese, and onions, they're pan-fried until golden brown and served with a side of sauerkraut or green salad.

- Mozartkugeln: These iconic chocolate marzipan balls, named after Salzburg's most famous son, are a must-try for any sweet tooth. The original Mozartkugeln, created by the Fürst confectionery in 1890, are still made by hand using a secret recipe. Their combination of smooth marzipan, rich nougat, and dark chocolate creates a decadent and unforgettable treat.

Recommended Restaurants:

- St. Peter Stiftskulinarium: Located within the historic St. Peter's Abbey, this restaurant offers a unique dining experience in a stunning setting. The menu features traditional Austrian dishes prepared with fresh, seasonal ingredients, and the wine list showcases a selection of Austrian and international wines.

- S'Nockerl im Elefantenhaus: This charming restaurant, housed in a historic building near the Salzburg Cathedral, is renowned for its Salzburger Nockerl. The menu also features other Austrian classics, as well as a selection of international dishes.

- Bärenwirt: This traditional Austrian inn, located just outside the city center, offers a cozy and authentic atmosphere. The menu features hearty dishes like Schweinsbraten (roast pork) and Backhendl (fried chicken), as well as a wide selection of Austrian beers and wines.

- Augustiner Bräustübl: This sprawling beer hall, located in the Mülln district, is a popular gathering place for locals and visitors alike. The self-service system allows you to choose from a variety of traditional Austrian dishes and enjoy them with a refreshing pint of Augustiner beer.

- Die Weisse: This Michelin-starred restaurant, located in the Hotel Goldener Hirsch, offers a refined dining experience with a focus on modern Austrian cuisine. The tasting menu showcases seasonal ingredients and innovative culinary techniques, creating a memorable gastronomic journey.

Beyond the Restaurants:

Salzburg's culinary scene extends beyond its restaurants. Explore the local markets, like the Grünmarkt and Schrannenmarkt, to discover fresh produce, artisanal cheeses, and regional specialties. Visit a traditional coffeehouse, like Café Tomaselli or Café Fürst, to savor a slice of Sachertorte (chocolate cake) and a cup of Viennese coffee. And don't forget to try a Mozartkugel or two from one of the many confectioneries throughout the city.

Tips for Foodies:

- Embrace the local specialties: Don't be afraid to try new and unfamiliar dishes. Salzburg's cuisine is full of surprises and delights.

- Explore the markets: The local markets offer a glimpse into Salzburg's culinary traditions and a chance to sample fresh, seasonal produce.

- Visit a coffeehouse: Experience the Viennese coffeehouse culture, a UNESCO-listed intangible cultural heritage.

- Make reservations: For popular restaurants, especially during peak season, it's advisable to make reservations in advance.

- Ask for recommendations: Don't hesitate to ask locals or your hotel concierge for recommendations on where to eat.

Salzburg's culinary scene is a reflection of its rich history, cultural influences, and passion for good food. By exploring its restaurants, markets, and coffeehouses, you'll embark on a gastronomic adventure that will leave you with a deeper appreciation for the city's flavors and traditions.

103 | SALZBURG TRAVEL GUIDE 2025

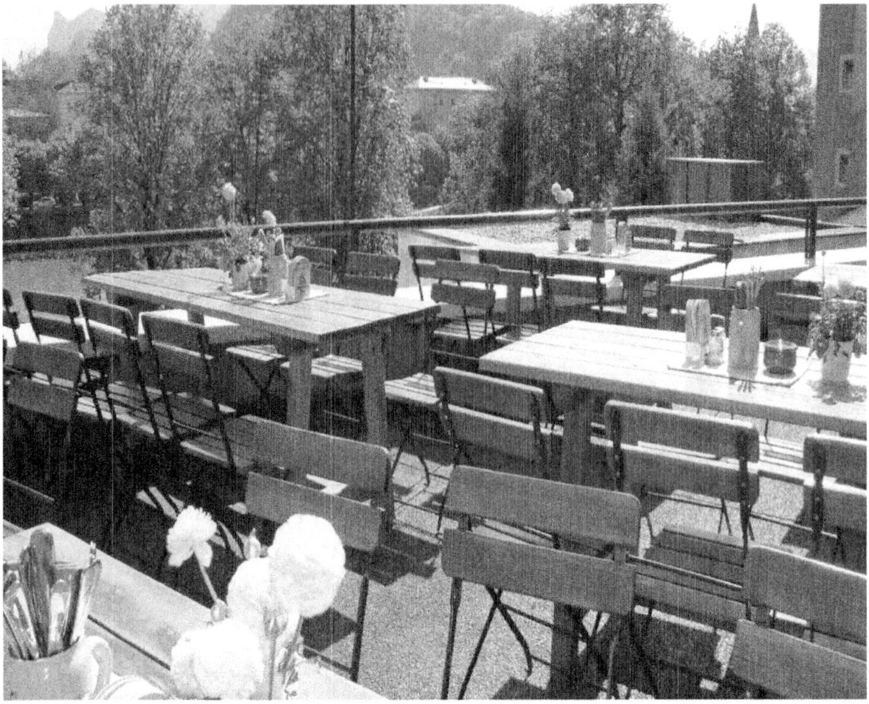

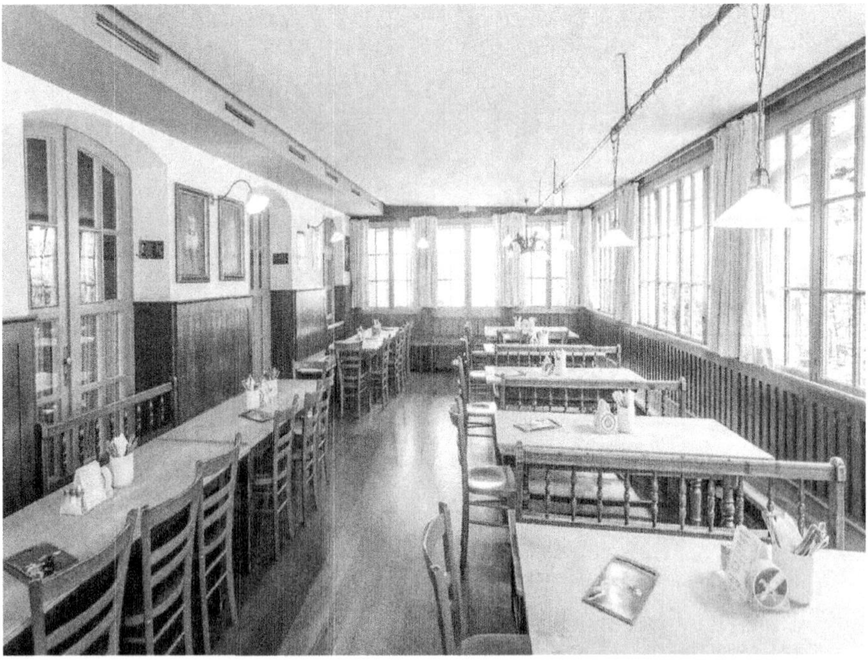

CHAPTER 5

Exploring Salzburg's Surroundings

Day Trip to Hallstatt

Nestled on the shores of a shimmering lake, amidst the dramatic backdrop of the Dachstein Mountains, Hallstatt is a fairytale village that seems plucked straight from the pages of a storybook. This UNESCO World Heritage site, renowned for its picturesque charm and breathtaking scenery, beckons travelers to step into a world of timeless beauty and tranquility.

A Journey through History:

Hallstatt's history dates back over 7,000 years, making it one of the oldest continuously inhabited settlements in Europe. Its strategic location, nestled between the mountains and the lake, and its rich salt deposits, have shaped its development and cultural identity.

The village's name, derived from the Celtic word "hall" meaning salt, reflects its deep connection to the salt mining industry that flourished here for centuries. The Hallstatt Salt Mine, one of the oldest in the world, offers a fascinating glimpse into this ancient industry and its impact on the region.

Architectural Treasures:

Hallstatt's charm lies in its harmonious blend of natural beauty and architectural heritage. Its quaint houses, built in the traditional Alpine style, cascade down the mountainside, their colorful facades reflecting in the lake's crystal-clear waters. Narrow alleyways, cobblestone streets, and flower-laden balconies create a picturesque ambiance that invites leisurely exploration.

The village's central square, Marktplatz, is a hub of activity, lined with cafes, shops, and historic landmarks. The 12th-century Catholic Church, with its slender spire and Gothic architecture, stands as a testament to Hallstatt's spiritual heritage. The nearby Beinhaus (Bone House), a unique ossuary, showcases a collection of intricately decorated skulls, a poignant reminder of the village's past.

Natural Splendors:

Hallstatt's natural setting is equally captivating. The Hallstätter See, a shimmering lake surrounded by majestic mountains, offers a breathtaking backdrop for outdoor activities and leisurely strolls. Boat tours provide a unique perspective on the village and its surroundings, while hiking trails lead to panoramic viewpoints and hidden waterfalls.

The nearby Dachstein Salzkammergut region, a UNESCO World Heritage site, boasts a wealth of natural wonders, from glaciers and ice caves to pristine lakes and alpine meadows. A visit to the Dachstein Skywalk, a glass-bottomed platform suspended over a 350-meter drop, offers a thrilling experience and unforgettable views.

Experiencing Hallstatt's Magic:

- Wander through the village: Take your time to explore Hallstatt's charming streets, admire its architecture, and soak in the peaceful atmosphere.

- Visit the Hallstatt Salt Mine: Delve into the depths of this ancient mine and learn about its history and significance.

- Take a boat tour: Enjoy a scenic boat ride on the Hallstätter See, admiring the village from a different perspective.

- Hike to the Skywalk: Challenge yourself with a hike to the Dachstein Skywalk for breathtaking panoramic views.

- Explore the Dachstein Salzkammergut region: Venture beyond Hallstatt to discover the natural wonders of this UNESCO World Heritage site.

- Savor local cuisine: Enjoy a meal at one of Hallstatt's restaurants, sampling regional specialties like fresh fish from the lake and hearty Austrian dishes.

Tips for a Day Trip from Salzburg:

- Transportation: The easiest way to reach Hallstatt from Salzburg is by train and bus. The journey takes approximately 2.5-3 hours each way. Consider purchasing a combination ticket that includes transportation and admission to the Salt Mine.
- Timing: Aim to arrive in Hallstatt early in the morning to avoid the crowds and enjoy a more peaceful experience.
- Duration: Allow at least 4-5 hours to explore Hallstatt, including a visit to the Salt Mine and a boat tour.
- Photography: Hallstatt is a photographer's paradise, so bring your camera to capture its beauty.
- Respect the locals: Remember that Hallstatt is a living community. Be respectful of the residents and their privacy.

A day trip to Hallstatt is a journey into a world of timeless beauty and tranquility. Its picturesque charm, rich history, and stunning natural scenery create an unforgettable experience. Whether you're seeking a romantic escape, a family adventure, or a solo exploration, Hallstatt will leave a lasting impression on your heart and soul.

Eagle's Nest and the Bavarian Alps

Venture beyond Salzburg's borders and immerse yourself in the breathtaking beauty of the Bavarian Alps, a realm of soaring peaks, emerald valleys, and pristine lakes. A highlight of this alpine adventure is a visit to the Eagle's Nest, a historic landmark perched atop the Kehlstein mountain, offering panoramic views that will leave you speechless.

The Eagle's Nest: A Controversial Legacy

The Eagle's Nest, or Kehlsteinhaus, was built in 1938 as a gift to Adolf Hitler on his 50th birthday. This mountaintop retreat, accessible only by a specially constructed road and an ornate brass elevator, served as a meeting place for Nazi officials and a symbol of their power. Despite its historical associations, the Eagle's Nest remains a popular tourist destination, offering stunning views and a glimpse into a controversial chapter of history.

A Journey to the Summit:

Reaching the Eagle's Nest is an adventure in itself. From the Obersalzberg bus terminal, you'll board a specially designed bus that navigates the winding mountain road with breathtaking precision. The final ascent is via a 124-meter-long brass-lined elevator that tunnels through the mountain, emerging onto a terrace with panoramic views.

Panoramic Vistas:

The Eagle's Nest's terrace offers a 360-degree panorama of the surrounding alpine landscape. On a clear day, you can see as far as Salzburg, the Salzkammergut Lake District, and even the distant peaks of the Austrian Alps. The view is truly awe-inspiring, a testament to the raw beauty and grandeur of nature.

Exploring the Bavarian Alps:

Beyond the Eagle's Nest, the Bavarian Alps beckon with a wealth of natural wonders and outdoor activities. Hiking trails wind through fragrant pine forests, leading to alpine meadows, crystal-clear lakes, and cascading waterfalls. The Königssee, a picturesque lake nestled amidst towering cliffs, offers boat tours and opportunities for swimming and kayaking.

The Berchtesgaden National Park, a UNESCO Biosphere Reserve, protects a diverse ecosystem of flora and fauna. Explore its trails, visit the historic salt mine, or take a cable car to the Jenner peak for even more spectacular views.

Tips for Visiting:

- Transportation: The easiest way to reach the Eagle's Nest from Salzburg is by organized tour or by renting a car. Allow at least half a day for the excursion, including travel time and exploration of the surrounding area.

- Tickets: Purchase tickets for the bus and elevator at the Obersalzberg bus terminal. It's advisable to book in advance, especially during peak season.

- Dress appropriately: The weather in the mountains can be unpredictable, so dress in layers and bring a jacket, even in summer. Wear comfortable shoes suitable for walking on uneven terrain.

- Respect the history: The Eagle's Nest is a historical site with a complex past. Be mindful of its significance and avoid any behavior that may be deemed disrespectful.

- Enjoy the views: Take your time to soak in the panoramic vistas from the Eagle's Nest terrace and the surrounding mountains.

A visit to the Eagle's Nest and the Bavarian Alps is an unforgettable experience that combines natural beauty, historical reflection, and outdoor adventure. Whether you're a history buff, a nature lover, or simply seeking breathtaking views, this excursion will leave a lasting impression on your heart and soul.

Sound of Music Tour

For generations, the iconic film "The Sound of Music" has captured hearts with its heartwarming story, unforgettable songs, and breathtaking scenery. A Sound of Music tour in Salzburg offers a unique opportunity to step into the world of the von Trapp family, relive the film's most memorable moments, and discover the city's connection to this beloved musical.

Following Maria's Footsteps:

A typical Sound of Music tour takes you on a journey through the picturesque landscapes and historic landmarks that served as the backdrop for the film. You'll visit iconic locations like:

- Mirabell Gardens: The scene of the Do-Re-Mi song, where Maria teaches the von Trapp children to sing, these beautifully manicured gardens offer a perfect blend of Baroque elegance and natural charm.

- Leopoldskron Palace: This majestic Rococo palace, with its stunning lakefront setting, served as the exterior of the von Trapp family home in the film. While the interior scenes were filmed elsewhere, the palace's grandeur and idyllic surroundings capture the essence of the von Trapp's privileged lifestyle.

- Hellbrunn Palace: The palace's trick fountains and gardens provided the backdrop for several scenes in the film, including the "Sixteen Going on Seventeen" gazebo scene and the "Do-Re-Mi" reprise. The palace's playful atmosphere and whimsical water features perfectly complement the film's lighthearted spirit.

- Nonnberg Abbey: This Benedictine abbey, perched atop a hill overlooking Salzburg, was where Maria lived as a postulant before becoming the von Trapp family's governess. The abbey's serene atmosphere and stunning views offer a glimpse into Maria's contemplative life before her fateful encounter with the von Trapp family.

- Mondsee Abbey: This picturesque abbey, located about 30 kilometers from Salzburg, served as the setting for the film's wedding scene between Maria and Captain von Trapp. Its Baroque architecture and serene surroundings create a romantic ambiance that perfectly captures the film's emotional climax.

Beyond the Film Locations:

A Sound of Music tour is more than just a sightseeing excursion. It's an opportunity to delve deeper into the film's historical context and its connection to Salzburg. Knowledgeable guides share fascinating insights into the von Trapp family's real-life story, the film's production, and its impact on Salzburg's tourism industry.

You'll also learn about the city's musical heritage and its role in shaping the film's iconic soundtrack. The songs, composed by Richard Rodgers and Oscar Hammerstein II, have become synonymous with Salzburg, their melodies echoing through its streets and concert halls.

Tips for Choosing a Tour:

- Duration: Tours typically range from half-day to full-day excursions, depending on the number of locations visited and the depth of information provided. Choose a tour that fits your schedule and interests.

- Transportation: Most tours include transportation in comfortable coaches or minibuses. Some tours also offer the option of cycling or hiking to certain locations.

- Guide: A knowledgeable and enthusiastic guide can enhance your experience by sharing interesting facts and stories about the film and its connection to Salzburg.

- Inclusions: Some tours include additional activities, such as a visit to the Salzburg Marionette Theatre for a puppet performance of "The Sound of Music" or a traditional Austrian lunch in a scenic setting.

- Price: Tour prices vary depending on the duration, inclusions, and operator. Compare different options to find a tour that fits your budget and preferences.

A Sound of Music tour is a must-do for any fan of the film or anyone seeking a unique and memorable way to experience Salzburg's beauty and cultural heritage. It's a journey that will transport you back in time, immersing you in the film's magic and leaving you with a deeper appreciation for its timeless story and unforgettable music.

Salzburg Lake District

Escape the city's hustle and bustle and immerse yourself in the tranquil embrace of the Salzburg Lake District (Salzburger Seenland), a picturesque region just a short drive north of Salzburg. This idyllic haven, characterized by its sparkling lakes, rolling hills, and charming villages, offers a refreshing retreat for nature lovers and outdoor enthusiasts. Whether you're seeking leisurely strolls, invigorating swims, or scenic hikes, the Salzburg Lake District promises a rejuvenating experience amidst breathtaking scenery.

A Tapestry of Lakes and Landscapes:

The Salzburg Lake District comprises four main lakes: Wallersee, Mattsee, Obertrumer See, and Grabensee. Each lake boasts its unique charm and allure, inviting you to explore its shores and discover its hidden treasures. The surrounding landscape, a harmonious blend of rolling hills, lush meadows, and dense forests, provides a picturesque backdrop for outdoor adventures and leisurely contemplation.

Activities for Every Taste:

The Salzburg Lake District offers a diverse range of activities to suit every preference and fitness level.

- Boating and Water Sports: Glide across the crystal-clear waters of the lakes on a leisurely boat tour, rent a kayak or paddleboard for an invigorating adventure, or try your hand at sailing or windsurfing. The calm waters and gentle breezes create ideal conditions for water-based activities.

- Swimming and Sunbathing: On warm summer days, the lakes' inviting waters beckon for a refreshing swim. Several lakeside beaches offer opportunities for sunbathing, picnicking, and relaxation. The Strandbad Seekirchen, located on the shores of Wallersee, is a popular spot with its sandy beach, playground, and water slide.

- Hiking and Biking: The region's network of trails caters to hikers and cyclists of all levels. Explore the gentle hillsides, wander through fragrant forests, or challenge yourself with a climb to a scenic viewpoint. The Mattsee-Wallersee circular trail offers a leisurely route with stunning lake views, while the more challenging Schafberg summit hike rewards you with panoramic vistas of the entire region.

- Exploring Charming Villages: The Salzburg Lake District is dotted with picturesque villages that exude traditional Austrian charm. Stroll through their cobblestone streets, admire their colorful houses, and visit their historic churches and castles. The villages of Mattsee, Seekirchen am Wallersee, and Obertrum am See are particularly noteworthy for their quaint ambiance and cultural attractions.

- Savoring Local Cuisine: The region's culinary scene reflects its agricultural heritage, with a focus on fresh, seasonal ingredients. Sample local specialties like freshly caught fish from the lakes, hearty Bauernkrapfen (farmer's doughnuts), and handcrafted cheeses. Numerous lakeside restaurants and cafes offer scenic dining experiences, allowing you to savor delicious meals while enjoying breathtaking views.

Tips for Exploring:

- Salzburg Card: If you're planning to visit multiple attractions in the region, consider purchasing the Salzburg

Card, which offers free admission to many museums and attractions, as well as discounts on public transportation.

- Public Transportation: The Salzburg Lake District is well-connected by public transportation, with regular bus and train services from Salzburg. Consider using these options to reduce your environmental impact and enjoy a stress-free journey.

- Bicycle Rentals: Several towns and villages offer bicycle rentals, allowing you to explore the region at your own pace and discover hidden gems off the beaten path.

- Seasonal Considerations: The Salzburg Lake District is beautiful year-round, but each season offers unique experiences. Summer is ideal for swimming, boating, and outdoor activities, while autumn showcases vibrant foliage and spring brings blooming flowers. Winter offers opportunities for ice skating and cross-country skiing.

The Salzburg Lake District is a haven of peace and natural beauty, offering a welcome contrast to the city's urban energy. Whether you're seeking outdoor adventure, cultural exploration, or simply a moment of quiet contemplation, this idyllic region will rejuvenate your senses and leave you with cherished memories.

Berchtesgaden National Park

Just a short journey from Salzburg lies a world of pristine wilderness and breathtaking beauty: Berchtesgaden National Park. This protected sanctuary, nestled amidst the majestic Bavarian Alps, is a haven for nature lovers, outdoor enthusiasts, and those seeking a respite from the urban hustle. Its diverse landscapes, abundant wildlife, and countless opportunities for adventure beckon you to explore its depths and discover its hidden treasures.

A Tapestry of Landscapes:

Berchtesgaden National Park is a tapestry of diverse landscapes, each offering its own unique charm and allure. From towering peaks and glacial valleys to crystal-clear lakes and emerald forests, the park's scenery is a feast for the eyes. The Watzmann, Germany's second-highest mountain, dominates the skyline, its rugged silhouette a testament to the forces of nature that shaped this region.

The Königssee, a picturesque lake nestled amidst towering cliffs, is a highlight of the park. Its emerald waters, reflecting the surrounding mountains, create a scene of unparalleled beauty. Boat tours offer a unique perspective on the lake's hidden coves and cascading waterfalls, while hiking trails lead to panoramic viewpoints and hidden gems.

Wildlife Encounters:

Berchtesgaden National Park is home to a rich diversity of wildlife, from majestic golden eagles soaring above the peaks to elusive chamois gracefully navigating the rocky terrain. Keep your eyes peeled for red deer, marmots, and a variety of alpine birds as you explore the park's trails. The park's commitment to conservation ensures that these creatures thrive in their natural habitat, offering visitors a chance to witness their beauty and grace firsthand.

Outdoor Adventures Await:

Berchtesgaden National Park is a playground for outdoor enthusiasts, offering a plethora of activities to suit all interests and fitness levels.

- Hiking: The park boasts over 260 kilometers of well-maintained hiking trails, ranging from gentle strolls to challenging climbs. The Wimbachklamm Gorge trail, with its dramatic rock formations and cascading waterfalls, is a popular choice, while the ascent to the Kehlsteinhaus (Eagle's Nest) offers both historical insights and breathtaking views.

- Biking: Mountain biking enthusiasts will find a network of trails winding through the park's diverse landscapes. Whether you prefer leisurely rides along the lakeshore or adrenaline-pumping descents through alpine terrain, there's a trail to suit your skill level.

- Climbing and Mountaineering: The park's towering peaks challenge experienced climbers and mountaineers, offering a thrilling test of skill and endurance. Guided tours and courses are available for those seeking professional instruction and support.

- Boating and Kayaking: The Königssee and other lakes within the park offer opportunities for boating, kayaking, and stand-up paddleboarding. Glide across the tranquil waters, soak in the scenery, and perhaps even enjoy a picnic lunch on a secluded lakeshore.

- Wildlife Watching: Observe the park's diverse wildlife in their natural habitat. Join a guided tour or explore the trails on your own, keeping your eyes peeled for signs of animal activity.

Tips for Exploring:

- Plan your visit: Berchtesgaden National Park is vast and diverse. Research the different areas and activities available to create an itinerary that suits your interests and time constraints.

- Respect nature: Stay on designated trails, avoid disturbing wildlife, and pack out all trash. Leave no trace of your visit.

- Check the weather: Mountain weather can be unpredictable, so dress in layers and be prepared for rain or snow.

- Inform others: Let someone know where you're going and when you expect to return, especially if you're venturing into remote areas.

- Guided tours: Consider joining a guided tour for a deeper understanding of the park's natural and cultural history.

Berchtesgaden National Park is a testament to the raw beauty and power of nature. Its diverse landscapes, abundant wildlife, and countless opportunities for adventure create an unforgettable experience. Whether you're seeking a challenging hike, a peaceful boat ride, or simply a moment of quiet contemplation amidst stunning scenery, Berchtesgaden will leave you with a renewed appreciation for the natural world.

123 | SALZBURG TRAVEL GUIDE 2025

124 | SALZBURG TRAVEL GUIDE 2025

CHAPTER 6

Practical Tips for First-Time Travelers

Getting Around Salzburg

Salzburg, with its compact city center and well-developed transportation network, is a joy to explore. Whether you prefer to stroll through its charming streets, hop on a bus or trolleybus, or rent a bicycle for a scenic ride, getting around Salzburg is easy and efficient.

Walking: The Best Way to Experience the City's Charm

- Compact City Center: Salzburg's historic center, a UNESCO World Heritage Site, is remarkably compact and pedestrian-friendly. Most major attractions, shops, and restaurants are within easy walking distance of each other.

- Scenic Strolls: Wander along the Salzach River, cross the picturesque footbridges, and lose yourself in the maze of cobblestone streets. You'll discover hidden courtyards, charming squares, and architectural gems at every turn.

- Walking Tours: Consider joining a guided walking tour to gain deeper insights into the city's history, culture, and landmarks. These tours offer a great way to orient yourself and learn about Salzburg's hidden treasures.

Public Transportation: Efficient and Convenient

- Salzburg Card: If you plan to use public transportation extensively, consider purchasing the Salzburg Card. This pass offers unlimited travel on buses and trolleybuses within the city, as well as free or discounted admission to many attractions.

- Buses and Trolleybuses: Salzburg's public transportation network is operated by Salzburg AG. Buses and trolleybuses cover the entire city and its surrounding areas, providing a convenient and affordable way to get around.

- Single Tickets and Day Passes: Single tickets can be purchased from bus drivers or ticket machines at major stops. Day passes offer unlimited travel for 24 hours and are a good value if you plan to use public transportation frequently.

- Route Planner: Use the Salzburg AG website or app to plan your journeys and find the best routes and schedules.

Biking: A Scenic and Eco-Friendly Option

- Bike Rentals: Several bike rental shops are located throughout Salzburg, offering a variety of bikes to suit different needs and preferences.

- Bike Paths: Salzburg boasts an extensive network of bike paths, making it easy and safe to explore the city and its surroundings on two wheels.

- Scenic Routes: Cycle along the Salzach River, explore the picturesque Hellbrunner Allee, or venture further afield to the Salzburg Lake District.

- Bike Tours: Consider joining a guided bike tour to discover hidden gems and learn about the city's history and culture from a local perspective.

Additional Tips for Getting Around:

- Download a map: A good map of Salzburg, either in print or digital format, will help you navigate the city with ease.

- Use a navigation app: Google Maps or other navigation apps can provide real-time directions and help you find your way around.

- Ask for help: If you're unsure about the best way to reach your destination, don't hesitate to ask locals or your hotel concierge for advice.

- Be mindful of pedestrians: Salzburg's streets can be crowded, especially during peak season. Be mindful of pedestrians and cyclists when walking or biking.

- Enjoy the journey: Getting around Salzburg is part of the experience. Take your time, savor the scenery, and embrace the city's unique charm.

With its compact size, pedestrian-friendly streets, and efficient public transportation network, Salzburg is a city that's easy to navigate and explore. Whether you choose to walk, bike, or take public transportation, you'll find getting around Salzburg to be a breeze. So, lace up your shoes, hop on a bike, or grab a bus ticket, and embark on your Salzburg adventure!

Money and Currency Exchange

As you prepare for your Salzburg adventure, understanding the local currency and financial practices is essential for a smooth and stress-free experience. Here's a comprehensive guide to money and currency exchange in Salzburg:

Currency:

- Euro (€): Austria is a member of the European Union and uses the euro (€) as its official currency. Euro banknotes come in denominations of 5, 10, 20, 50, 100, 200, and 500, while coins are available in 1, 2, 5, 10, 20, and 50 cent denominations, as well as €1 and €2 coins.

Currency Exchange:

- Best Exchange Rates: Generally, you'll get the best exchange rates by using your debit or credit card at an ATM in Salzburg. Avoid exchanging currency at the airport or train station, as these locations often have higher fees and less favorable rates.

- Currency Exchange Offices: If you need to exchange cash, several currency exchange offices (Wechselstuben) can be found throughout the city center. Compare rates and fees before exchanging your money.

- Credit Cards: Major credit cards, such as Visa and Mastercard, are widely accepted in Salzburg. However, it's always a good idea to carry some cash for smaller purchases or in case of emergencies.

ATMs:

- Bankomats: ATMs, locally known as Bankomats, are readily available throughout Salzburg. Look for ATMs affiliated with major banks, as these typically offer the best exchange rates and lower fees.

- Fees: Your bank may charge a foreign transaction fee for ATM withdrawals. Check with your bank before traveling to understand the fees associated with using your card abroad.

- Security: Be cautious when using ATMs, especially at night or in secluded areas. Cover your PIN when entering it and be aware of your surroundings.

Tipping:

- Restaurants: Tipping is customary in Salzburg restaurants. A 10% tip is generally considered appropriate for good service. If you're particularly pleased with the service, you can leave a slightly larger tip.

- Cafes and Bars: Round up the bill to the nearest euro or leave a small amount of change as a tip.

- Taxis: Round up the fare to the nearest euro or leave a small tip.

- Hotels: A tip of €1-2 per bag is customary for bellhops. You can also leave a small tip for housekeeping staff at the end of your stay.

- Other Services: Tipping is not expected for other services, such as hairdressers or tour guides. However, if you're particularly happy with the service, you can leave a small tip.

Additional Tips for a Smooth Financial Experience:

- Notify your bank: Inform your bank of your travel plans to avoid any issues with using your card abroad.

- Carry a mix of cash and cards: Having both cash and cards on hand provides flexibility and ensures you can make purchases even if one payment method is unavailable.

- Check your receipts: Always review your receipts carefully to ensure you're charged the correct amount.

- Be mindful of exchange rates: Keep track of the current exchange rate to ensure you're getting a fair deal when exchanging currency or making purchases.

- Budget wisely: Salzburg can be an expensive city, especially during peak season. Create a budget before your trip and stick to it to avoid overspending.

By following these tips and being mindful of local financial practices, you can ensure a smooth and enjoyable financial experience during your Salzburg adventure. With your finances in order, you can focus on exploring the city's many treasures and creating unforgettable memories.

Safety and Security

Salzburg enjoys a reputation as a safe and welcoming city, where visitors can explore with peace of mind. However, as with any destination, it's essential to exercise common sense and take precautions to ensure a worry-free experience.

Addressing Common Concerns:

- Petty Theft: While Salzburg has a low crime rate, petty theft, such as pickpocketing and bag snatching, can occur, especially in crowded areas like tourist attractions and public transportation.

- Scams: Be wary of scams targeting tourists, such as overpriced souvenirs, fake taxi drivers, or individuals offering unsolicited assistance.

- Solo Female Travelers: Salzburg is generally safe for solo female travelers, but it's advisable to take extra precautions, such as avoiding walking alone at night and staying in well-lit areas.

Tips for Staying Safe:

- Be aware of your surroundings: Pay attention to your surroundings and avoid distractions like using your phone while walking.

- Keep valuables secure: Keep your valuables, such as your passport, money, and electronics, in a secure location, like a hotel safe or a money belt worn under your clothing.

- Use caution in crowded areas: Be extra vigilant in crowded areas, where pickpockets may operate. Keep your bags close to your body and avoid carrying large amounts of cash.

- Travel in groups: If possible, travel with companions, especially at night or in unfamiliar areas.

- Trust your instincts: If you feel uncomfortable in a particular situation or location, trust your instincts and leave.

- Report any incidents: If you experience any problems or become a victim of a crime, report it to the local police immediately.

Emergency Contacts:

- Police: 133
- Ambulance: 144
- Fire Department: 122
- European Emergency Number: 112

Additional Safety Tips:

- Travel insurance: Purchase comprehensive travel insurance that covers medical emergencies, trip cancellations, and lost or stolen belongings.

- Copy important documents: Make copies of your passport, visa, and other important documents, and store them in a separate location.

- Register with your embassy: If you're from a country with an embassy or consulate in Austria, consider registering your travel plans with them. This can be helpful in case of emergencies or natural disasters.

- Learn basic German phrases: Knowing a few basic German phrases can help you communicate with locals and navigate the city more easily.

- Respect local customs: Familiarize yourself with Austrian customs and etiquette to avoid offending locals and ensure a positive experience.

Salzburg is a safe and welcoming city where visitors can relax and enjoy their stay. By following these simple tips and exercising common sense, you can ensure a worry-free visit and focus on creating unforgettable memories.

Local Customs and Etiquette

As you immerse yourself in Salzburg's enchanting atmosphere, understanding and respecting local customs and etiquette is key to fostering positive interactions with the locals and ensuring a culturally enriching experience. While Austrians are generally welcoming and accommodating, familiarizing yourself with their social norms will enhance your understanding of their culture and help you navigate social situations with ease.

Greetings and Introductions:

- Formal Greetings: When meeting someone for the first time, a firm handshake and direct eye contact are customary. Use the formal address "Herr" (Mr.) or "Frau" (Mrs./Ms.) followed by their last name until invited to use their first name.

- Titles and Academic Degrees: Austrians place great importance on titles and academic degrees. Address people using their appropriate titles, such as "Doktor" (Dr.) or "Professor," followed by their last name.

- Greetings in Shops and Public Spaces: It's considered polite to greet people when entering a shop, restaurant, or other public space with a simple "Guten Tag" (Good day) or "Grüß Gott" (literally "Greet God," a common greeting in Austria and Bavaria).

Social Interactions:

- Punctuality: Austrians value punctuality, so arrive on time for appointments, meetings, and social gatherings.

- Politeness and Respect: Maintain a polite and respectful demeanor when interacting with locals. Avoid loud or boisterous behavior, especially in public spaces.

- Personal Space: Austrians generally appreciate personal space, so avoid standing too close or touching people unnecessarily.

- Dining Etiquette: When dining in restaurants, wait to be seated and avoid moving chairs or tables without permission. It's considered polite to keep your hands visible on the table while eating.

- Gift-Giving: If you're invited to someone's home, it's customary to bring a small gift, such as flowers, chocolates, or a bottle of wine.

Public Behavior:

- Queueing: Austrians generally form orderly queues, so wait your turn patiently and avoid cutting in line.

- Public Transportation: Be mindful of other passengers on public transportation. Offer your seat to elderly or disabled individuals and avoid loud conversations or music.

- Smoking: Smoking is prohibited in most public places, including restaurants, bars, and public transportation.

- Photography: Ask for permission before taking photos of people, especially in religious or private settings.

- Noise: Avoid making excessive noise, especially late at night or in residential areas.

Additional Tips:

- Learn a few basic German phrases: While many Austrians speak English, learning a few basic German phrases, such as "Guten Tag," "Danke," and "Bitte," will be appreciated and help you connect with locals.

- Be mindful of cultural sensitivities: Avoid discussing sensitive topics, such as politics or religion, unless you're familiar with the person and their views.

- Dress appropriately: Austrians tend to dress conservatively, especially in formal settings. When visiting churches or attending cultural events, dress modestly and avoid wearing revealing clothing.

- Embrace the local culture: Show an interest in Austrian culture and traditions, and be open to new experiences.

By following these tips and embracing Salzburg's local customs and etiquette, you'll foster respectful interactions with locals and create a more enriching and enjoyable travel experience. Remember, a little cultural sensitivity goes a long way in building bridges and creating positive memories.

Language Basics

While many Austrians, especially in tourist areas, speak English fluently, learning a few basic German phrases can significantly enhance your travel experience in Salzburg. It demonstrates respect for the local culture, facilitates smoother interactions with locals, and can even open doors to unexpected encounters and deeper connections.

Essential Greetings and Phrases:

- Guten Tag: Good day (formal)
- Grüß Gott: Greet God (informal, common in Austria and Bavaria)
- Hallo: Hello (informal)
- Auf Wiedersehen: Goodbye (formal)
- Tschüss: Bye (informal)

- Bitte: Please
- Danke: Thank you
- Entschuldigung: Excuse me/Sorry
- Ja: Yes
- Nein: No
- Sprechen Sie Englisch?: Do you speak English?
- Ich verstehe nicht: I don't understand.
- Können Sie das bitte wiederholen?: Could you please repeat that?
- Wie viel kostet das?: How much does this cost?
- Wo ist die Toilette?: Where is the toilet?

Additional Useful Phrases:

- Ich möchte ein Bier, bitte: I would like a beer, please.
- Ich möchte einen Kaffee, bitte: I would like a coffee, please.
- Ich habe eine Reservierung: I have a reservation.
- Die Rechnung, bitte: The bill, please.
- Hilfe!: Help!

Pronunciation Tips:

- German pronunciation can be challenging for English speakers. Pay attention to the vowel sounds, which are often different from English.

- Practice the phrases before your trip, so you can pronounce them confidently and naturally.

- Don't be afraid to make mistakes. Most Austrians will appreciate your effort to speak their language, even if your pronunciation isn't perfect.

Beyond the Basics:

If you have time, consider learning a few more phrases or even taking a beginner German course before your trip. This will enable you to have more meaningful interactions with locals and gain a deeper appreciation for the culture.

Resources:

- Phrasebooks and language apps: Several phrasebooks and language apps, such as Duolingo and Babbel, can help you learn basic German phrases and vocabulary.

- Online resources: Many websites and videos offer German language lessons and pronunciation guides.

- Local language schools: If you're staying in Salzburg for an extended period, consider enrolling in a German language course at a local language school.

Remember, even a few basic phrases can go a long way in enhancing your travel experience in Salzburg. So, embrace the challenge, practice your German, and enjoy the rewards of connecting with locals and immersing yourself in the culture.

142 | SALZBURG TRAVEL GUIDE 2025

143 | SALZBURG TRAVEL GUIDE 2025

144 | SALZBURG TRAVEL GUIDE 2025

CHAPTER 7

Salzburg for Specific Interests

Salzburg for Families

Salzburg, with its blend of history, culture, and natural beauty, offers a wealth of experiences that will captivate and delight families of all ages. From interactive museums and playful attractions to scenic outdoor adventures and family-friendly accommodations, this enchanting city has something to offer every member of your clan. Let's explore the many ways Salzburg can create cherished memories for your family vacation.

Family-Friendly Attractions:

- Haus der Natur: This natural history museum is a wonderland of discovery, featuring interactive exhibits on dinosaurs, animals, minerals, and the human body. Kids will love exploring the aquarium, the reptile zoo, and the science center, while adults can appreciate the museum's comprehensive collection and educational displays.

- Salzburg Zoo: Home to over 1,200 animals from around the world, Salzburg Zoo offers a fun and educational experience for the whole family. Wander through its spacious enclosures and observe lions, tigers, elephants, giraffes, and many other fascinating creatures. The zoo also features a petting zoo, playgrounds, and picnic areas, making it a perfect day out for families.

- Spielzeug Museum: This toy museum is a nostalgic trip down memory lane for adults and a source of endless fascination for children. Its collection spans centuries, showcasing antique dolls, teddy bears, model trains, and other playthings that evoke the joy and wonder of childhood.

- Hohensalzburg Fortress: This imposing medieval fortress, perched atop a hill overlooking the city, offers stunning views and a glimpse into Salzburg's history. Kids will love exploring its ramparts, towers, and dungeons, while adults can appreciate its architectural grandeur and historical significance. The fortress funicular provides a fun and scenic way to reach the top.

- Sound of Music Tour: Relive the magic of the iconic film with a family-friendly Sound of Music tour. Visit the movie's filming locations, sing along to its unforgettable songs, and learn about the von Trapp family's real-life story.

Outdoor Adventures:

- Hellbrunn Palace and Trick Fountains: This Renaissance palace, with its playful trick fountains, is a guaranteed hit with kids and adults alike. Wander through the gardens, discover hidden water features, and enjoy a picnic lunch amidst the scenic surroundings.

- Untersberg Cable Car: Take a scenic cable car ride to the summit of the Untersberg mountain for breathtaking panoramic views of Salzburg and the surrounding Alps. On a clear day, you can see as far as the Dachstein glacier and the Bavarian plains. The mountaintop also offers hiking trails and a restaurant with stunning vistas.

- Salzburg Lake District: This picturesque region, just a short drive from Salzburg, offers a variety of outdoor activities for families. Enjoy a leisurely boat ride on one of the lakes, swim in the crystal-clear waters, or hike through the surrounding hills and forests.

- Horse-Drawn Carriage Rides: Take a romantic horse-drawn carriage ride through Salzburg's Old Town, admiring its Baroque architecture and charming streets from a unique perspective.

Family-Friendly Accommodations:

- Hotel & Villa Auersperg: This family-run hotel offers spacious apartments and suites, a playground, and a swimming pool, making it a comfortable and convenient choice for families.

- MEININGER Hotel Salzburg City Center: This modern hotel offers a mix of family rooms, dorms, and private rooms, all with en-suite bathrooms. Its central location and amenities like a guest kitchen and laundry facilities make it a popular choice for budget-minded families.

- Jugendgästehaus Salzburg: This youth hostel offers affordable accommodation in a central location. It features family rooms, a playground, and a games room, making it a great option for families on a budget.

Additional Tips for Families:

- Plan your itinerary: Research family-friendly activities and attractions in advance and create an itinerary that suits your children's ages and interests.

- Pack snacks and drinks: Keep kids energized and hydrated by packing snacks and drinks for your outings.

- Embrace flexibility: Be prepared to adjust your plans based on your children's needs and energy levels.

- Take advantage of family discounts: Many attractions and transportation providers offer discounts for families. Inquire about these options when booking tickets or planning your activities.

- Enjoy the simple pleasures: Some of the best family memories are made during simple moments, like strolling through a park, enjoying a picnic lunch, or playing a game together in your hotel room.

Salzburg is a city that welcomes families with open arms. Its diverse attractions, scenic surroundings, and family-friendly accommodations create an ideal setting for a memorable vacation. By embracing its childlike wonder and playful spirit, you'll create cherished memories that will last a lifetime.

Salzburg for Couples

Salzburg, with its enchanting blend of history, culture, and natural beauty, sets the stage for a truly romantic getaway. Whether you're seeking intimate moments amidst stunning scenery, indulging in culinary delights, or exploring hidden corners hand-in-hand, this captivating city offers a wealth of experiences to create a memorable trip for couples.

Romantic Experiences:

- Stroll through Mirabell Gardens: Wander hand-in-hand through the meticulously manicured gardens of Mirabell Palace, recreating the iconic "Do-Re-Mi" scene from "The Sound of Music." The fragrant blooms, ornate fountains, and panoramic views of the Hohensalzburg Fortress create an idyllic setting for romance.

- Sunset at Mönchsberg: Ascend the Mönchsberg hill at dusk and witness a breathtaking sunset over Salzburg. The panoramic vistas of the city's rooftops, spires, and the distant Alps create a magical ambiance that's perfect for sharing a special moment.

- Horse-Drawn Carriage Ride: Embark on a romantic horse-drawn carriage ride through Salzburg's Old Town, snuggling close as you admire the city's Baroque architecture and charming streets. The gentle clip-clop of hooves and the soft glow of lanterns add to the enchanting atmosphere.

- Mozart Dinner Concert: Indulge in a unique evening of music and cuisine at a Mozart Dinner Concert. Enjoy a delicious three-course meal while listening to live performances of Mozart's most beloved works in a historic setting, such as St. Peter Stiftskeller or the Baroque Hall of Mirabell Palace.

- Salzburg Festival: If you're visiting during the summer months, consider attending a performance at the world-renowned Salzburg Festival. The festival's diverse program offers something for every taste, from opera and theater to classical music concerts.

Intimate Restaurants:

- Goldener Hirsch Restaurant: This Michelin-starred restaurant, located in the historic Hotel Goldener Hirsch, offers a refined dining experience in an elegant setting. The menu features innovative interpretations of classic Austrian dishes, prepared with seasonal ingredients and paired with a selection of fine wines.

- St. Peter Stiftskulinarium: This historic restaurant, nestled within the walls of St. Peter's Abbey, exudes old-world charm and romantic ambiance. The menu showcases traditional Austrian cuisine, prepared with fresh, local ingredients, and the candlelit tables create an intimate setting for a special evening.

- Restaurant m32: Perched atop the Mönchsberg hill, this stylish restaurant offers breathtaking views of Salzburg and a menu that blends Austrian and international flavors. The panoramic windows and terrace seating create a romantic atmosphere that's perfect for couples.

- Triangel: This cozy restaurant, tucked away in a quiet corner of the Old Town, offers a relaxed and intimate setting. The menu features creative dishes inspired by Mediterranean and Asian cuisine, prepared with fresh, seasonal ingredients.

- Imlauer Sky Bar & Restaurant: Located on the top floor of the Imlauer Hotel Pitter Salzburg, this rooftop bar and restaurant offers stunning panoramic views of the city and the surrounding mountains. It's the perfect spot for a romantic sunset cocktail or a special dinner under the stars.

Scenic Spots:

- Kapuzinerberg: This wooded hill, located across the Salzach River from the Old Town, offers a peaceful escape from the city's hustle and bustle. Hike to the summit for panoramic views, explore the Capuchin Monastery, or simply enjoy a quiet picnic amidst the greenery.

- Hellbrunn Palace Gardens: Wander hand-in-hand through the enchanting gardens of Hellbrunn Palace, discovering hidden fountains, romantic grottoes, and scenic pathways.

- Salzburg Lake District: Take a day trip to the Salzburg Lake District and enjoy a leisurely boat ride on one of its picturesque lakes, surrounded by stunning mountain scenery.

- Salzburg Old Town at Night: As the sun sets, Salzburg's Old Town transforms into a magical wonderland, with its illuminated landmarks and cobblestone streets creating a romantic ambiance.

Additional Tips for Couples:

- Take a cooking class: Learn to prepare traditional Austrian dishes together in a fun and interactive cooking class.

- Visit a local winery: Sample regional wines and enjoy a romantic picnic in a vineyard setting.

- Attend a concert or opera: Experience the magic of live music at one of Salzburg's many concert halls or theaters.

- Take a leisurely bike ride: Rent bicycles and explore the city's scenic bike paths, enjoying the fresh air and beautiful scenery.

- Simply relax and enjoy each other's company: Salzburg's laid-back atmosphere and stunning surroundings provide the perfect backdrop for quality time together.

Salzburg is a city that inspires romance and creates lasting memories. By embracing its beauty, culture, and culinary delights, couples can ignite sparks and create a truly special experience.

Whether you're celebrating a special occasion or simply seeking a romantic getaway, Salzburg is the perfect destination to fall in love all over again.

Salzburg for Solo Travelers

Salzburg, with its welcoming atmosphere, compact size, and wealth of attractions, is an ideal destination for solo travelers seeking both cultural immersion and independent exploration. Embracing the freedom of solo travel allows you to set your own pace, discover hidden gems, and connect with fellow adventurers from around the globe.

Navigating Salzburg Independently:

- Embrace the Walkable City: Salzburg's historic center, a UNESCO World Heritage Site, is remarkably compact and pedestrian-friendly, making it easy to navigate on foot. Wander through its charming streets, discover hidden alleyways, and stumble upon unexpected delights.

- Utilize Public Transportation: Salzburg boasts an efficient public transportation network, with buses and trolleybuses connecting all major attractions and neighborhoods. Consider purchasing the Salzburg Card for unlimited travel and discounted admission to many sites.

- Rent a Bicycle: Explore Salzburg's scenic surroundings on two wheels. Several bike rental shops offer a variety of bikes to suit different preferences, and the city's extensive network of bike paths makes cycling a safe and enjoyable experience.

Activities for Solo Adventurers:

- Immerse Yourself in Culture: Salzburg's vibrant cultural scene offers a plethora of activities for solo travelers. Visit the Salzburg Museum to delve into the city's rich history, attend a concert or opera at the Mozarteum or the Felsenreitschule, or enjoy a traditional puppet show at the Salzburg Marionette Theatre.

- Explore Nature's Beauty: Venture beyond the city center and discover the natural wonders surrounding Salzburg. Hike through the scenic trails of Mönchsberg or Kapuzinerberg, take a boat tour on the Salzach River, or embark on a day trip to the breathtaking Salzkammergut Lake District or the majestic Berchtesgaden National Park.

- Indulge in Culinary Delights: Salzburg's gastronomic scene caters to all tastes and budgets. Savor traditional Austrian cuisine at a cozy inn, enjoy a coffee and pastry at a historic café, or sample local delicacies at a bustling market. Don't miss the opportunity to try the iconic Salzburger Nockerl or the delectable Mozartkugeln.

- Join a Group Tour or Activity: While solo travel offers freedom and flexibility, joining a group tour or activity can be a great way to meet fellow travelers and share experiences. Consider a Sound of Music tour, a cooking class, or a guided hike to connect with like-minded individuals.

- Embrace the Nightlife: Salzburg's nightlife scene, while not as vibrant as some larger cities, offers a variety of options for solo travelers. Enjoy a drink at a traditional beer hall, listen to live music at a cozy bar, or catch a performance at a local theater.

Social Opportunities:

- Hostels and Guesthouses: Staying in hostels or guesthouses provides opportunities to meet other solo travelers and share tips and experiences. Many hostels organize social events, such as walking tours or game nights, creating a friendly and welcoming atmosphere.

- Language Exchange Meetups: Join a language exchange meetup to practice your German skills and connect with locals and other travelers. These events offer a relaxed and informal setting for conversation and cultural exchange.

- Shared Tours and Activities: As mentioned earlier, participating in group tours or activities is a great way to meet people and make new friends.

- Online Communities and Apps: Several online communities and apps, such as Meetup and Couchsurfing, connect travelers with similar interests and provide opportunities for social interaction.

- Be Open and Approachable: Don't be afraid to strike up conversations with locals or other travelers. A friendly smile and a willingness to engage can lead to meaningful connections and enriching experiences.

Tips for Solo Travelers:

- Plan Ahead: Research your destination thoroughly, including safety tips, transportation options, and recommended activities.

- Stay Connected: Keep your phone charged and carry a portable charger. Consider purchasing a local SIM card or using a Wi-Fi hotspot to stay connected.

- Trust Your Instincts: If you feel uncomfortable in a particular situation or location, trust your gut feeling and leave.

- Be Confident and Independent: Embrace the freedom of solo travel and enjoy exploring Salzburg at your own pace.

- Stay Open to New Experiences: Be open to meeting new people, trying new things, and stepping outside your comfort zone.

Solo travel in Salzburg can be an empowering and enriching experience. By following these tips and embracing the city's welcoming atmosphere, you'll create unforgettable memories and discover the joys of independent exploration.

Salzburg for Budget Travelers

Salzburg, with its reputation as a cultural and historical gem, might seem like a destination reserved for those with deep pockets. However, with a bit of savvy planning and resourcefulness, budget-conscious travelers can also experience the city's magic without sacrificing quality or enjoyment. Here are some tips and recommendations to help you make the most of your Salzburg adventure on a budget:

Accommodation:

- Hostels: Salzburg boasts a selection of clean and comfortable hostels offering dormitory-style and private rooms at affordable rates. YoHo International Youth

Hostel, located centrally, provides a vibrant social atmosphere and convenient access to attractions.

- Guesthouses and Pensions: These family-run establishments offer a more personal touch and often include breakfast in the room rate. Look for options slightly outside the city center for better value, like Pension Adlerhof or Pension Elisabeth.

- Camping: For the adventurous, camping is an excellent budget-friendly option. Camping Schloss Aigen, situated in a picturesque park setting, offers a range of camping and caravan facilities within easy reach of the city center.

- Apartment Rentals: Consider renting an apartment for a longer stay, as it can be more cost-effective than staying in a hotel. Websites like Airbnb and Booking.com offer a variety of options to suit different budgets and group sizes.

Dining:

- Imbiss Stände: These street food stalls, scattered throughout the city, offer quick and delicious bites at affordable prices. Try a classic Bosna sausage, a Leberkäse roll, or a hearty pretzel.

- University Mensa: The Mensa, or student cafeteria, at the University of Salzburg offers budget-friendly meals for everyone, not just students. Enjoy a variety of hot dishes, salads, and desserts at significantly lower prices than in traditional restaurants.

- Supermarkets and Bakeries: Stock up on snacks and drinks at local supermarkets like SPAR or Billa. Grab a freshly baked pastry or sandwich from a bakery for a quick and affordable breakfast or lunch on the go.

- Picnic in the Park: Pack a picnic lunch and enjoy it in one of Salzburg's beautiful parks, like Mirabell Gardens or the Volksgarten. It's a great way to save money and soak up the city's atmosphere.

Activities:

- Free Walking Tours: Several companies offer free walking tours of Salzburg, providing an informative and entertaining introduction to the city's history and landmarks. Tips are appreciated but not mandatory.

- Hike Mönchsberg or Kapuzinerberg: These scenic hills offer breathtaking views of the city and surrounding mountains, and access is completely free. Pack a picnic and enjoy a leisurely afternoon surrounded by nature.

- Salzburg Card: If you plan to visit multiple attractions, the Salzburg Card can be a worthwhile investment. It offers free admission to many museums and attractions, as well as discounts on public transportation.

- Student Discounts: If you're a student, take advantage of student discounts offered at many museums, theaters, and other attractions.

- Free Concerts and Events: Throughout the year, Salzburg hosts a variety of free concerts and events, particularly during the summer months. Check local listings for details.

Additional Tips:

- Travel Off-Season: Consider visiting Salzburg during the shoulder seasons (spring or autumn) or even in winter to avoid peak season crowds and higher prices.

- Cook Your Own Meals: If your accommodation has a kitchen, consider preparing some of your meals to save on dining expenses.

- Utilize Public Transportation: Salzburg's public transportation system is efficient and affordable. Purchase a day pass or Salzburg Card for unlimited travel.

- Walk or Bike: Salzburg is a compact city, so take advantage of its walkability and bike-friendly infrastructure to explore at your own pace.

- Seek Out Free Activities: Many of Salzburg's parks, gardens, and churches are free to enter. Take advantage of these opportunities to experience the city's beauty and culture without spending a dime.

By following these tips and embracing a spirit of adventure, you can experience the magic of Salzburg without breaking the bank. Remember, the most valuable travel experiences often come from exploring off the beaten path, connecting with locals, and appreciating the simple pleasures that the city has to offer.

Salzburg for Luxury Travelers

For discerning travelers seeking the pinnacle of indulgence and exclusivity, Salzburg offers a curated collection of high-end experiences, luxurious accommodations, and world-class dining options. Embrace the city's refined charm as you immerse yourself in its rich cultural heritage, savor its culinary masterpieces, and pamper yourself with impeccable service and lavish surroundings.

Luxurious Accommodations:

- Hotel Sacher Salzburg: This iconic hotel, synonymous with Viennese elegance, offers a haven of luxury overlooking the Salzach River. Its opulent rooms and suites, adorned with exquisite furnishings and antiques, provide a haven of tranquility and sophistication. Indulge in the hotel's Michelin-starred restaurant, unwind in its spa, and enjoy the attentive service that defines the Sacher experience.

- Hotel Goldener Hirsch, a Luxury Collection Hotel: Nestled in the heart of the Old Town, this historic hotel seamlessly blends tradition and contemporary luxury. Its elegant rooms and suites, featuring antique furnishings and modern amenities, offer a refined retreat amidst the city's vibrant energy. Savor exquisite cuisine at its Michelin-starred restaurant and experience the personalized service that makes this hotel a favorite among discerning travelers.

- Schloss Mönchstein Hotel: Perched atop a hill overlooking Salzburg, this castle hotel offers breathtaking views and an ambiance of secluded luxury. Its spacious suites, adorned with original artwork and antiques, provide a regal escape from the everyday. Relax in the hotel's spa, enjoy a candlelit dinner on its terrace, and immerse yourself in the tranquility of its surroundings.

High-End Experiences:

- Private Sound of Music Tour: Embark on a personalized journey through the iconic film's locations with a private Sound of Music tour. Your dedicated guide will share insider stories and insights, tailoring the experience to your interests and preferences.

- Helicopter Tour of the Alps: Soar above the breathtaking landscapes of the Salzburg region on a private helicopter tour. Witness the majesty of the Alps from a bird's-eye view, capturing unforgettable memories and panoramic photographs.

- VIP Salzburg Festival Experience: Indulge in the ultimate Salzburg Festival experience with VIP access to exclusive events, backstage tours, and meet-and-greets with renowned artists. Enjoy premium seating at performances and savor gourmet cuisine in private lounges.

- Private Shopping Experience: Discover Salzburg's finest boutiques and ateliers with a personal shopper who will curate a bespoke shopping experience tailored to your style and preferences.

- Hot Air Balloon Ride: Float above the picturesque landscapes of Salzburg and its surroundings on a romantic hot air balloon ride. Witness the sunrise or sunset from a unique vantage point and create unforgettable memories with your loved one.

World-Class Dining:

- Ikarus at Hangar-7: This Michelin-starred restaurant, located within the Red Bull Hangar-7 complex, offers a truly unique dining experience. Its monthly changing menu features guest chefs from around the world, showcasing their culinary artistry and pushing the boundaries of gastronomy.

- Senns.Restaurant: This Michelin-starred restaurant, located in the Hotel Goldener Hirsch, serves refined Austrian cuisine with a modern twist. Its elegant ambiance and impeccable service create a memorable dining experience.

- The Glass Garden: This stylish restaurant, located in the Hotel Schloss Mönchstein, offers breathtaking views of Salzburg and a menu that blends international flavors with regional ingredients. Its sophisticated ambiance and panoramic windows create a romantic and memorable setting.

- Carpe Diem Finest Fingerfood: This Michelin-starred restaurant offers a unique culinary concept, serving a series of small, artfully presented dishes that showcase the chef's creativity and passion for flavor.

Additional Tips for Luxury Travelers:

- **Book in Advance:** Salzburg's high-end experiences and accommodations are in high demand, especially during peak season. Book your reservations well in advance to avoid disappointment.

- **Embrace the City's Cultural Heritage:** Salzburg's rich cultural offerings provide ample opportunities for indulgence. Attend a classical music concert, visit the Salzburg Museum, or explore the city's Baroque architecture and art collections.

- **Pamper Yourself:** Treat yourself to a spa treatment, a private yoga session, or a personal shopping experience. Salzburg offers a variety of ways to relax and rejuvenate in style.

- **Hire a Private Guide:** Enhance your experience by hiring a private guide who can tailor your itinerary to your interests and preferences, providing insider knowledge and access to exclusive experiences.

- **Savor the Moment:** Salzburg's timeless beauty and refined ambiance invite you to slow down and appreciate the finer things in life. Take your time to explore, indulge, and create lasting memories in this enchanting city.

Salzburg offers a wealth of luxurious experiences for discerning travelers seeking the pinnacle of indulgence and exclusivity. By embracing its refined charm, immersing yourself in its cultural heritage, and pampering yourself with its high-end offerings, you'll create a truly unforgettable journey that will leave you feeling refreshed, inspired, and utterly spoiled.

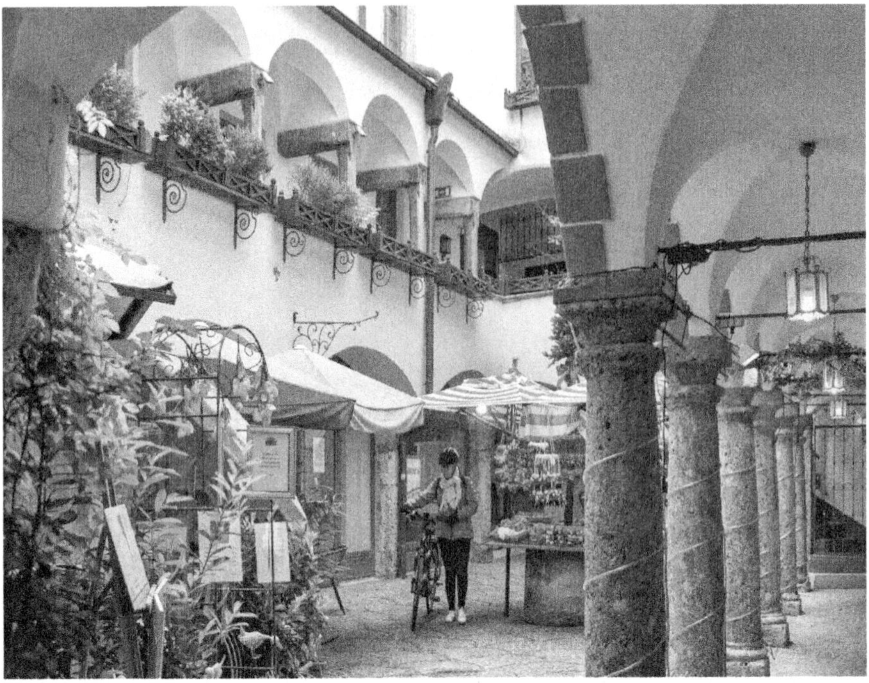

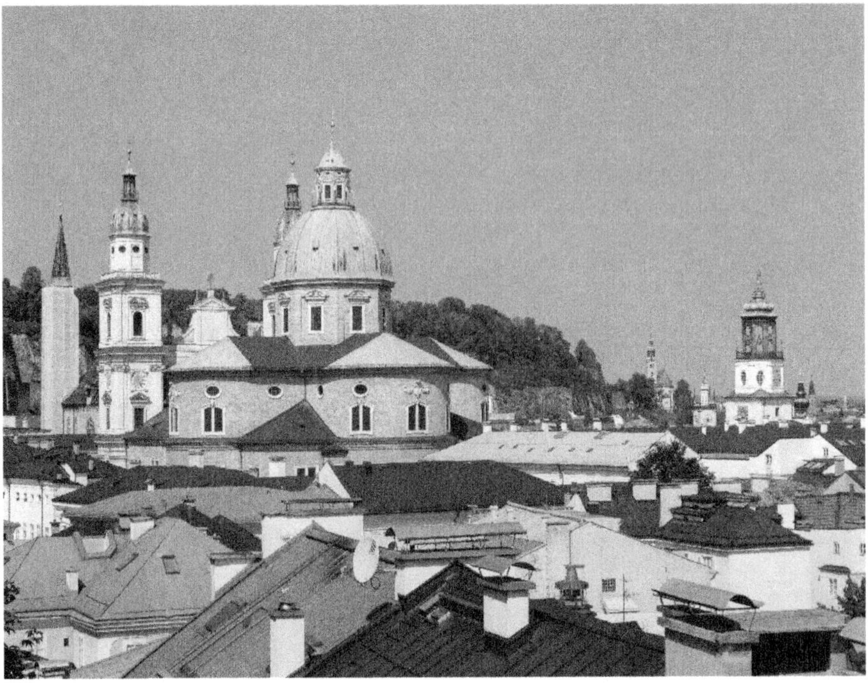

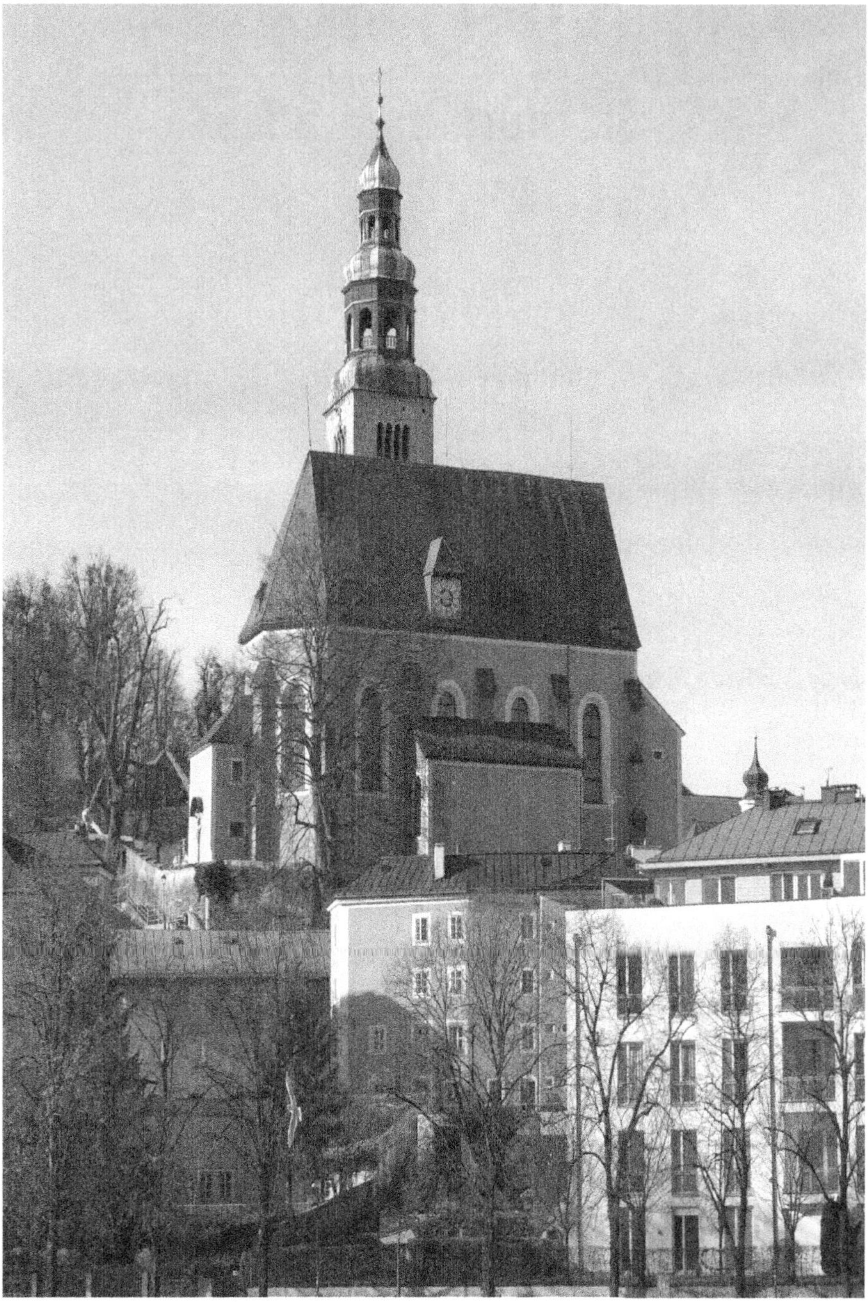

CHAPTER 8

Salzburg Itineraries

3-Day Itinerary

Salzburg, a city brimming with historical and cultural treasures, can captivate even within a short visit. This three-day itinerary offers a well-paced exploration of its must-see landmarks and essential experiences, allowing you to savor the city's essence while leaving ample room for personal discoveries.

Day 1: Unveiling the Historic Heart

- Morning:
    - Start your day with a leisurely stroll through Mirabell Gardens, immersing yourself in its Baroque elegance and "Sound of Music" charm.
    - Next, venture into the heart of the Old Town (Altstadt), a UNESCO World Heritage Site. Explore the bustling Getreidegasse, admire Mozart's birthplace, and marvel at the grandeur of the Salzburg Cathedral.
- Afternoon:

- Ascend to the Hohensalzburg Fortress, either by foot or the convenient funicular, and be rewarded with panoramic views of the city and surrounding landscapes. Take time to explore the fortress's museums and courtyards, delving into its rich history.
- In the afternoon, enjoy a leisurely boat ride on the Salzach River, admiring the city's skyline from a different perspective.

- Evening:
  - Conclude your day with a Mozart Dinner Concert, savoring a delicious meal while listening to live performances of Mozart's masterpieces in a historic setting.
  - Alternatively, stroll through the illuminated streets of the Old Town, enjoying its enchanting ambiance and perhaps catching a performance at a local theater or music venue.

Day 2: Cultural Immersion and Scenic Delights

- Morning:
  - Visit Mozart's Residence, gaining insights into the composer's life and creative process.

- - Next, explore the Salzburg Museum, delving deeper into the city's history and cultural heritage through its diverse collection of artifacts and interactive exhibits.
- Afternoon:
  - Escape the city's hustle and bustle with a visit to Hellbrunn Palace and its whimsical trick fountains. Delight in the playful water features, explore the palace's gardens, and enjoy a leisurely picnic lunch.
- Evening:
  - Immerse yourself in Salzburg's vibrant cultural scene with a performance at the Salzburg Marionette Theatre, where puppets bring classic operas and plays to life with astonishing artistry.
  - For a more contemporary experience, check out the program at the Salzburg State Theatre or the Felsenreitschule, a unique open-air theater carved into the Mönchsberg cliff face.

Day 3: Nature's Embrace and Personal Exploration

- Morning:
  - Embark on a scenic hike up the Mönchsberg or Kapuzinerberg, enjoying breathtaking views of the city and surrounding mountains.

- Alternatively, take a leisurely bike ride along the Salzach River or explore the picturesque Hellbrunner Allee.

- Afternoon:
  - Dedicate the afternoon to personal exploration, revisiting your favorite spots or discovering new hidden gems.
  - Consider a visit to one of Salzburg's lesser-known museums, such as the Toy Museum or the DomQuartier, or simply wander through the charming streets of the Old Town, soaking up its unique atmosphere.

- Evening:
  - Conclude your Salzburg adventure with a farewell dinner at a traditional Austrian restaurant, savoring local specialties and reflecting on the cherished memories you've created.
    - If time permits, catch a final performance at a local music venue or enjoy a drink at a cozy bar, toasting to your unforgettable experience in Mozart's city.

This three-day itinerary offers a glimpse into Salzburg's multifaceted charm, combining historical exploration, cultural immersion, and scenic delights. While it highlights the must-see landmarks, it also leaves room for personal discoveries and serendipitous encounters, allowing you to create your own unique Salzburg story. Remember, this is just a suggestion, and you can customize it to suit your interests and preferences.

With its compact size and efficient transportation network, Salzburg is easy to navigate and explore, even within a short timeframe. Embrace its welcoming atmosphere, savor its cultural riches, and let its timeless beauty leave an indelible mark on your heart and soul.

5-Day Itinerary

With five days in Salzburg, you can embark on a more immersive journey, venturing beyond the must-see landmarks to discover hidden gems and experience the natural beauty of the surrounding region. This itinerary offers a balanced blend of cultural exploration, outdoor adventure, and personal discovery, allowing you to create a truly memorable Salzburg experience.

Day 1: Historical Immersion and Baroque Splendor

- Morning:
    - Begin your day with a leisurely stroll through Mirabell Gardens, taking in its manicured lawns, ornate

fountains, and stunning views of the Hohensalzburg Fortress.

- o Next, venture into the heart of the Old Town (Altstadt), a UNESCO World Heritage Site. Explore the Getreidegasse, a charming shopping street lined with traditional shops and historic buildings, including Mozart's Birthplace.
- o Visit the Salzburg Cathedral, a Baroque masterpiece that dominates the city's skyline. Admire its grandeur, architectural details, and artistic treasures.

- Afternoon:
  - o Ascend to the Hohensalzburg Fortress, Salzburg's iconic landmark, offering breathtaking panoramic views of the city and surrounding landscapes. Explore its museums, courtyards, and ramparts, immersing yourself in its rich history.
  - o In the afternoon, enjoy a guided walking tour of the Old Town, delving deeper into its historical and cultural significance. Discover hidden alleyways, charming squares, and architectural gems that might otherwise go unnoticed.

- Evening:

- Treat yourself to a Mozart Dinner Concert, savoring a delicious meal while listening to live performances of Mozart's masterpieces in a historic setting.
- Alternatively, stroll through the illuminated streets of the Old Town, enjoying its enchanting ambiance and perhaps catching a performance at a local theater or music venue.

Day 2: Unveiling Hidden Gems and Artistic Expressions

- Morning:
  - Visit Mozart's Residence, gaining insights into the composer's life and creative process during his time in Salzburg. Explore the museum's exhibits, showcasing original furnishings, musical instruments, and personal belongings.
  - Next, discover the hidden gem of St. Peter's Abbey and Cemetery, a tranquil oasis in the heart of the city. Wander through its picturesque cemetery, admire its Baroque architecture, and perhaps enjoy a meal at the historic St. Peter Stiftskeller.
- Afternoon:
  - Immerse yourself in Salzburg's vibrant cultural scene with a visit to the Salzburg Museum. Explore its diverse

collection of artifacts, artworks, and interactive exhibits, gaining a deeper understanding of the city's history and heritage.
  - In the afternoon, take a leisurely stroll through the charming Nonntal district, known for its traditional houses, hidden courtyards, and local atmosphere.
- Evening:
  - Experience the magic of the Salzburg Marionette Theatre, where puppets bring classic operas and plays to life with astonishing artistry.
  - Alternatively, catch a performance at the Salzburg State Theatre or the Felsenreitschule, a unique open-air theater carved into the Mönchsberg cliff face.

Day 3: A Fairytale Escape to Hallstatt

- Full Day:
  - Embark on a day trip to the enchanting lakeside village of Hallstatt, a UNESCO World Heritage site renowned for its picturesque charm and breathtaking scenery.
  - Explore its narrow alleyways, admire its traditional houses, and visit its historic landmarks, including the Hallstatt Salt Mine and the Beinhaus (Bone House).

- Take a boat tour on the Hallstätter See, enjoying panoramic views of the village and surrounding mountains.
- Hike to a scenic viewpoint for a bird's-eye perspective of this fairytale setting.
- Savor a delicious meal at a lakeside restaurant, sampling local specialties and soaking up the tranquil atmosphere.

Day 4: Alpine Adventure and Panoramic Vistas

- Full Day:
  - Venture into the Bavarian Alps for a day of natural beauty and historical reflection.
  - Visit the Eagle's Nest, a historic landmark perched atop the Kehlstein mountain, offering breathtaking panoramic views of the surrounding alpine landscape.
  - Explore the Berchtesgaden National Park, hiking through its scenic trails, admiring its pristine lakes, and observing its diverse wildlife.
  - Take a boat tour on the Königssee, a picturesque lake nestled amidst towering cliffs.

- Enjoy a traditional Bavarian meal at a mountain hut or restaurant, savoring the flavors of the region.

Day 5: Personal Exploration and Farewell

- Morning:
    - Dedicate the morning to personal exploration, revisiting your favorite spots or discovering new hidden gems. Consider a leisurely bike ride along the Salzach River, a visit to a local market, or a coffee break at a charming café.

- Afternoon:
    - Purchase souvenirs and gifts for loved ones, capturing the essence of your Salzburg experience.
    - Relax and reflect on your journey, savoring the memories you've created and the experiences you've shared.

- Evening:
    - Enjoy a farewell dinner at a restaurant of your choice, celebrating your Salzburg adventure and toasting to future travels.

- Take a final stroll through the illuminated streets of the Old Town, bidding adieu to this enchanting city and its timeless allure.

This five-day itinerary offers a more immersive experience of Salzburg and its surroundings, allowing you to delve deeper into its cultural treasures, natural wonders, and hidden gems. While it's a packed itinerary, it also allows for flexibility and personal exploration, ensuring a fulfilling and memorable journey tailored to your interests and preferences.

7-Day Itinerary

With seven days at your disposal, immerse yourself in the multifaceted allure of Salzburg and its picturesque surroundings. This itinerary seamlessly blends cultural exploration, natural immersion, and leisurely moments, creating a symphony of experiences that will resonate long after your journey concludes.

Day 1: Unveiling Salzburg's Historic Heart

- Morning: Embark on a guided walking tour of the Old Town (Altstadt), a UNESCO World Heritage Site, delving into its rich history and architectural marvels. Explore the bustling Getreidegasse, admire Mozart's birthplace, and marvel at the grandeur of the Salzburg Cathedral.

- Afternoon: Ascend to the Hohensalzburg Fortress, either by foot or the convenient funicular, and be rewarded with breathtaking panoramic views. Explore the fortress's museums, courtyards, and ramparts, immersing yourself in its storied past.

- Evening: Indulge in a Mozart Dinner Concert, savoring a delectable meal while listening to live performances of Mozart's masterpieces. Alternatively, stroll through the illuminated streets of the Old Town, enjoying its enchanting ambiance.

Day 2: Cultural Immersion and Artistic Expressions

- Morning: Visit Mozart's Residence, gaining insights into the composer's life and creative process. Next, discover the hidden gem of St. Peter's Abbey and Cemetery, a tranquil oasis in the heart of the city.

- Afternoon: Immerse yourself in Salzburg's vibrant cultural scene with a visit to the Salzburg Museum. Explore its diverse collection and interactive exhibits, gaining a deeper understanding of the city's history and heritage.

- Evening: Experience the magic of the Salzburg Marionette Theatre, where puppets bring classic operas and plays to life. Alternatively, catch a performance at the Salzburg

State Theatre or the Felsenreitschule, a unique open-air theater.

Day 3: A Fairytale Escape to Hallstatt

- Full Day: Embark on a day trip to the enchanting lakeside village of Hallstatt. Explore its narrow alleyways, admire its traditional houses, and visit the Hallstatt Salt Mine and the Beinhaus. Take a boat tour on the Hallstätter See, enjoying panoramic views, and savor a meal at a lakeside restaurant.

Day 4: Alpine Adventure and Panoramic Vistas

- Full Day: Venture into the Bavarian Alps for a day of natural beauty. Visit the Eagle's Nest, perched atop the Kehlstein mountain, for breathtaking views. Explore the Berchtesgaden National Park, hiking its scenic trails and admiring its pristine lakes. Take a boat tour on the Königssee and enjoy a traditional Bavarian meal.

Day 5: Leisurely Delights and Personal Exploration

- Morning: Unwind with a leisurely breakfast at a charming café, savoring local pastries and coffee. Take a scenic bike ride along the Salzach River or explore the picturesque Hellbrunner Allee, enjoying the fresh air and natural beauty.

- Afternoon: Dedicate the afternoon to personal exploration, revisiting your favorite spots or discovering new hidden gems. Consider a visit to one of Salzburg's lesser-known museums, a leisurely stroll through a local market, or a relaxing afternoon in a spa.

- Evening: Treat yourself to a fine dining experience at a renowned restaurant, savoring Salzburg's culinary delights. Alternatively, enjoy a performance at a local music venue or simply unwind with a drink at a cozy bar, reflecting on your journey thus far.

Day 6: Sound of Music and Cultural Enrichment

- Morning: Embark on a Sound of Music tour, reliving the magic of the iconic film and visiting its filming locations in and around Salzburg. Sing along to the unforgettable songs and learn about the von Trapp family's real-life story.

- Afternoon: Delight in the whimsical surprises of Hellbrunn Palace and its trick fountains. Wander through the gardens, discover hidden water features, and enjoy the palace's playful atmosphere.

- Evening: Attend a classical music concert or opera at the Mozarteum or the Felsenreitschule, immersing yourself in Salzburg's rich musical heritage.

Day 7: Farewell to Salzburg and Future Adventures

- Morning: Purchase souvenirs and gifts for loved ones, capturing the essence of your Salzburg experience. Enjoy a final leisurely stroll through the Old Town, revisiting your favorite spots and bidding farewell to this enchanting city.
- Afternoon: Depart from Salzburg, carrying cherished memories and a newfound appreciation for its beauty, culture, and history.

This seven-day itinerary offers a comprehensive exploration of Salzburg and its surroundings, balancing cultural immersion, natural beauty, and moments of relaxation. With its flexibility and ample opportunities for personal discovery, it allows you to create a truly unique and unforgettable Salzburg experience.

Themed Itineraries

Salzburg's allure extends beyond its general appeal, offering a wealth of experiences tailored to specific interests. Whether you're a music enthusiast, a history buff, or an outdoor adventurer, these themed itineraries will guide you to the heart of your passions, ensuring a fulfilling and personalized journey.

1. **For the Music Lover: A Melodic Odyssey**

Mozart concert in Salzburg

- Day 1: Arrive in Salzburg and immerse yourself in the city's musical heritage with a visit to Mozart's Birthplace and Residence. In the evening, attend a Mozart Dinner Concert, savoring a delectable meal while listening to live performances of his masterpieces.

- Day 2: Explore the Mozarteum Foundation Salzburg, a renowned music institution dedicated to preserving and promoting Mozart's legacy. Attend a concert or masterclass, and visit the Mozarteum's museum to delve deeper into the composer's life and work.

- Day 3: Embark on a Sound of Music tour, reliving the magic of the iconic film and visiting its filming locations in and around Salzburg. In the evening, enjoy a performance at the Salzburg Marionette Theatre, where puppets bring Mozart's operas to life with astonishing artistry.

- Day 4: Attend a concert or opera at the prestigious Salzburg Festival, experiencing the pinnacle of musical excellence in a world-renowned setting. Alternatively, explore the city's vibrant music scene by visiting smaller venues and discovering local talent.

- Day 5: Take a day trip to the picturesque village of St. Gilgen, Mozart's mother's birthplace, and visit the Mozart

Haus museum. In the evening, enjoy a leisurely dinner at a traditional restaurant, perhaps accompanied by live music.

2. For the History Buff: A Journey Through Time

- Day 1: Begin your exploration of Salzburg's rich history with a guided walking tour of the Old Town, a UNESCO World Heritage Site. Visit the Salzburg Cathedral, a Baroque masterpiece, and the imposing Hohensalzburg Fortress, a medieval stronghold offering panoramic views.

- Day 2: Delve deeper into Salzburg's past at the Salzburg Museum, where interactive exhibits and artifacts chronicle the city's evolution from a Roman settlement to a modern European city. In the afternoon, explore the Residenzplatz and the Salzburg Residenz, the former palace of the prince-archbishops.

- Day 3: Embark on a day trip to the medieval town of Berchtesgaden, Germany, and visit the Eagle's Nest, a historic landmark perched atop the Kehlstein mountain. Learn about its controversial past and enjoy breathtaking views of the surrounding Alps.

- Day 4: Discover the hidden gem of St. Peter's Abbey and Cemetery, one of the oldest continuously inhabited monasteries in the German-speaking world. Explore its

Baroque church, picturesque cemetery, and fascinating catacombs.

- Day 5: Visit the Celtic Museum Hallein, located in a former salt mine, to learn about the region's ancient history and the importance of salt mining in Salzburg's development. In the evening, enjoy a traditional Austrian meal at a historic restaurant, immersing yourself in the city's culinary heritage.

3. **For the Outdoor Adventurer: Embracing Nature's Playground**

- Day 1: Start your active adventure with a scenic hike up the Mönchsberg or Kapuzinerberg, enjoying breathtaking views of Salzburg and the surrounding mountains. In the afternoon, rent a bicycle and explore the city's picturesque bike paths, following the Salzach River or venturing into the surrounding countryside.

- Day 2: Embark on a day trip to the stunning Salzkammergut Lake District, a UNESCO World Heritage site renowned for its pristine lakes, rolling hills, and charming villages. Enjoy a boat ride on one of the lakes, hike to a scenic viewpoint, or simply relax on a lakeside beach.

- Day 3: Venture into the Bavarian Alps for a day of hiking and exploration in the Berchtesgaden National Park. Choose from a variety of trails, ranging from gentle strolls to challenging climbs, and immerse yourself in the park's natural beauty.

- Day 4: Take a scenic cable car ride to the summit of the Untersberg mountain for panoramic views of Salzburg and the surrounding Alps. Enjoy a hike along the mountaintop trails or simply relax and savor the breathtaking scenery.

- Day 5: Explore the city's surroundings on a guided kayaking or rafting tour on the Salzach River. Alternatively, try your hand at rock climbing or paragliding for an adrenaline-fueled adventure.

These themed itineraries offer a starting point for tailoring your Salzburg experience to your specific interests. Remember, these are just suggestions, and you can customize them further to create a truly personalized journey.

Whether you're a music lover, a history buff, or an outdoor enthusiast, Salzburg has something special to offer. Embrace its diverse attractions, immerse yourself in its rich culture, and create unforgettable memories that will last a lifetime.

CHAPTER 9

Salzburg Off the Beaten Path

Non-Touristy Neighborhoods

While Salzburg's Old Town captivates with its iconic landmarks and bustling energy, venturing beyond the city center reveals a tapestry of charming neighborhoods that offer a glimpse into the city's authentic soul. These lesser-known enclaves, where locals go about their daily lives and traditions thrive, invite you to step off the tourist trail and experience a more intimate and genuine side of Salzburg.

Mülln: A Haven of Creativity and Bohemian Spirit

Just across the Salzach River from the Old Town, Mülln beckons with its artistic flair and laid-back vibe. This vibrant neighborhood, once a working-class district, has transformed into a hub of creativity, attracting artists, musicians, and students. Stroll through its colorful streets, adorned with street art and murals, and discover a plethora of independent shops, cafes, and galleries.

- **Augustiner Bräustübl:** This sprawling beer garden, a beloved institution among locals, is a must-visit for its convivial atmosphere and traditional Bavarian fare. Grab a Maß (liter-sized mug) of Augustiner beer, find a seat at one of the long wooden tables, and mingle with the locals as you savor hearty pretzels and sausages.

- **Atelierhaus Salzburg:** This former tobacco factory, now a vibrant arts complex, houses studios, galleries, and performance spaces. Explore its exhibitions, attend a concert or workshop, and immerse yourself in Salzburg's contemporary art scene.

Nonntal: A Tranquil Retreat with Historic Charm

Nestled at the foot of the Mönchsberg hill, Nonntal exudes a sense of tranquility and old-world charm. This residential neighborhood, known for its picturesque streets, Baroque architecture, and verdant gardens, offers a peaceful escape from the city's hustle and bustle.

- **Nonnberg Abbey:** Perched atop the hill, this Benedictine abbey offers stunning views of Salzburg and a glimpse into the city's spiritual heritage. Explore its Baroque church, wander through its peaceful gardens, and perhaps even catch a glimpse of the nuns who call this place home.

- **Villa Trapp:** This elegant villa, once home to the real-life von Trapp family, is now a hotel and restaurant. Enjoy a meal on its terrace, surrounded by lush greenery, and imagine the von Trapp children singing their way through its halls.

Aigen: A Leafy Suburb with Artistic Flair

Located south of the city center, Aigen is a leafy suburb known for its elegant villas, sprawling parks, and artistic community. This tranquil neighborhood offers a welcome respite from the tourist crowds, inviting you to slow down and savor its peaceful ambiance.

- **Schloss Leopoldskron:** This magnificent Rococo palace, nestled on the shores of a lake, served as the exterior of the von Trapp family home in "The Sound of Music." While the interior is not open to the public, its gardens and lakeside setting are worth exploring.
- **Salzburg Open-Air Museum:** This sprawling museum showcases traditional rural architecture and crafts from across the Salzburg region. Wander through its reconstructed farmhouses, workshops, and mills, gaining insights into the region's rich cultural heritage.

Gneis: A Hidden Gem with Local Flavor

Tucked away on the eastern bank of the Salzach River, Gneis is a hidden gem that offers a glimpse into Salzburg's local life. This residential neighborhood, known for its quaint streets, traditional houses, and lively atmosphere, is a great place to experience the city's authentic charm.

- **Gneis Moarhof:** This historic farmhouse, now a cultural center, hosts a variety of events throughout the year, including concerts, exhibitions, and workshops. It's a great place to connect with the local community and experience Salzburg's vibrant cultural scene.

- **Local Cafes and Restaurants:** Gneis is home to several charming cafes and restaurants where you can savor traditional Austrian cuisine and mingle with locals. Try the Gasthof Wilder Mann for hearty dishes and a cozy atmosphere, or Café Wernbacher for coffee and pastries in a relaxed setting.

Tips for Exploring Salzburg's Non-Touristy Neighborhoods:

- Venture beyond the Old Town: Don't be afraid to step outside the city center and explore Salzburg's diverse neighborhoods.

- Use public transportation: Salzburg's efficient public transportation network makes it easy to reach different parts of the city.

- Talk to locals: Strike up conversations with locals to get insider tips on hidden gems and off-the-beaten-path experiences.

- Embrace the unexpected: Be open to serendipitous encounters and spontaneous discoveries.

- Savor the local flavor: Sample the cuisine, visit the markets, and experience the unique atmosphere of each neighborhood.

By venturing beyond the tourist hotspots, you'll discover a side of Salzburg that few visitors get to experience. These non-touristy neighborhoods offer a glimpse into the city's authentic soul, its vibrant culture, and its warm hospitality. Embrace the opportunity to explore these hidden gems and create your own unique Salzburg story.

Lesser-Known Museums and Galleries

While Salzburg boasts world-renowned cultural institutions like the Salzburg Museum and the Mozarteum, a treasure trove of lesser-known museums and galleries awaits those seeking a deeper dive into the city's artistic scene. These hidden gems, often tucked away in quiet corners or showcasing niche collections, offer a unique perspective on Salzburg's creative spirit and provide a platform for emerging artists and alternative artistic expressions.

Museums:

- Museum of Modern Art Mönchsberg (Museum der Moderne Salzburg Mönchsberg): Perched atop the Mönchsberg hill, this contemporary art museum boasts a striking architectural presence and panoramic city views. Its collection spans a range of artistic movements, showcasing works by renowned artists like Picasso, Warhol, and Lichtenstein, as well as emerging Austrian and international talents. The museum's rooftop terrace and café offer a delightful setting for contemplation and conversation.

- Museum of Modern Art Rupertinum (Museum der Moderne Salzburg Rupertinum): Located in a historic building in the heart of the Old Town, this museum complements its Mönchsberg counterpart with a focus on Austrian and international contemporary art. Its exhibitions showcase a diverse range of media, from painting and sculpture to photography and video installations, providing a dynamic and thought-provoking experience.

- Salzburg Barockmuseum: Housed in the magnificent Mirabell Palace, this museum delves into the artistic and cultural flourishing of the Baroque era in Salzburg. Its collection includes paintings, sculptures, furniture, and decorative arts that showcase the opulence and grandeur of this period, offering insights into the lives and tastes of the prince-archbishops and their court.

- Spielzeug Museum (Toy Museum): This delightful museum, located in the Bürgerspital building, takes visitors on a nostalgic journey through the world of childhood. Its collection spans centuries, showcasing antique dolls, teddy bears, model trains, and other playthings that evoke the joy and wonder of childhood.

- Salzburg Panorama Museum: This unique museum houses a 360-degree panorama painting of Salzburg, created in 1829 by Johann Michael Sattler. This remarkable artwork, measuring 26 meters in length, offers a detailed and immersive view of the city as it appeared in the 19th century.

Galleries:

- Galerie Thaddaeus Ropac: This internationally renowned gallery, with branches in Salzburg and Paris, showcases contemporary art by established and emerging artists. Its exhibitions feature a diverse range of media and artistic styles, pushing boundaries and challenging conventional notions of art.

- Galerie Fotohof: This gallery, dedicated to contemporary photography, showcases works by Austrian and international photographers. Its exhibitions explore a variety of themes and techniques, offering a glimpse into the diverse world of photographic art.

- Periscope Gallery: This artist-run space, located in the Andräviertel district, provides a platform for emerging artists to showcase their work. Its exhibitions feature a range of media and artistic styles, offering a glimpse into the cutting edge of Salzburg's contemporary art scene.

- Salzburger Kunstverein: This non-profit art association promotes contemporary art through exhibitions, events, and educational programs. Its gallery space showcases works by local, national, and international artists, offering a dynamic and engaging platform for artistic dialogue.

Tips for Exploring Salzburg's Lesser-Known Museums and Galleries:

- Check opening hours and admission fees: These institutions often have limited opening hours and varying admission fees. Check their websites or social media pages for up-to-date information.

- Allow ample time: Plan your visits carefully, allowing sufficient time to appreciate the artworks and exhibits at each location.

- Join a guided tour: Some museums and galleries offer guided tours, providing deeper insights into their collections and artistic context.

- Attend events and openings: Many museums and galleries host special events, artist talks, and exhibition openings, offering opportunities for interaction and engagement with the local art scene.

- Support local artists: Consider purchasing artwork or merchandise from local galleries and artists, contributing to the city's vibrant creative community.

By venturing beyond the well-trodden tourist path, you'll discover a side of Salzburg's artistic scene that's often overlooked. These lesser-known museums and galleries offer a unique perspective on the city's cultural heritage and provide a platform for emerging artists and alternative artistic expressions. Embrace the opportunity to explore these hidden gems and expand your understanding of Salzburg's creative spirit.

Local Events and Festivals

Beyond its world-renowned cultural events, Salzburg boasts a vibrant calendar of local festivals and seasonal celebrations that offer a unique window into the city's community life and traditions. These gatherings, often steeped in history and brimming with local flavor, invite you to immerse yourself in Salzburg's authentic charm and experience its festive spirit firsthand.

Springtime Delights:

- Osterfestspiele Salzburg (Salzburg Easter Festival): As the city awakens from its winter slumber, the Salzburg Easter Festival heralds the arrival of spring with a series of world-class classical music concerts and opera performances. This prestigious event, held during Holy Week, attracts renowned artists and music lovers from around the globe, filling Salzburg's concert halls with sublime melodies and captivating performances.

- Rupertikirtag: In late September, Salzburg honors its patron saint, Saint Rupert, with a lively folk festival that dates back centuries. The streets around the cathedral come alive with colorful stalls selling traditional crafts, regional delicacies, and festive trinkets. Live music, folk dancing, and traditional costumes add to the vibrant atmosphere, creating a joyful celebration of Salzburg's heritage.

Summer Vibes:

- Sommer Szene Salzburg: This contemporary arts festival, held in July, showcases a diverse program of theater, dance, and performance art. Embrace the city's creative spirit as you witness innovative productions, engage in thought-provoking discussions, and experience the cutting edge of Salzburg's cultural scene.

- Jazz & The City: In late October, Salzburg's streets and squares transform into stages for a vibrant jazz festival. Talented musicians from around the world fill the air with improvisational melodies, creating a lively and spontaneous atmosphere that's perfect for tapping your feet and letting loose.

- Jedermann: This iconic play, performed annually during the Salzburg Festival, is a must-see for any visitor. Written by Hugo von Hofmannsthal and first performed in 1920, Jedermann tells the allegorical tale of a wealthy man confronted with his mortality. Its powerful message and stunning setting in front of the Salzburg Cathedral make it an unforgettable experience.

Autumnal Hues:

- Bauernherbst (Harvest Festival): As the leaves turn golden and the air crisp, the Salzburg Lake District celebrates the harvest season with a series of festive events. Bauernherbst markets showcase local produce, handcrafted goods, and traditional cuisine, while folk music and dancing add to the festive spirit.

- Salzburger Bergadvent: During the Advent season, the Salzburg mountains come alive with the magic of Christmas. This traditional Advent market, held in the picturesque village of Großarl, features handcrafted ornaments, festive treats, and heartwarming Glühwein. Enjoy the festive atmosphere, surrounded by snow-capped peaks and twinkling lights.

Winter Wonderland:

- Christkindlmarkt (Christmas Market): Salzburg's most famous Christmas market, held on Residenzplatz, transforms the city center into a winter wonderland. Stroll through its charming stalls, adorned with festive decorations, and discover a treasure trove of handcrafted ornaments, traditional toys, and culinary delights. Warm up with a cup of Glühwein, listen to carolers singing festive tunes, and embrace the spirit of the season.

- Mozart Week: Held in late January and early February, this prestigious festival celebrates the life and legacy of Salzburg's most famous son, Wolfgang Amadeus Mozart. Immerse yourself in the world of classical music with a series of concerts, operas, and chamber music performances featuring world-renowned artists.

Tips for Experiencing Local Events:

- Check the Calendar: Consult the Salzburg tourism website or local event listings for up-to-date information on upcoming events and festivals.

- Plan Ahead: Some events, especially popular festivals like the Salzburg Festival, require advance ticket purchases. Plan your visit accordingly to ensure you don't miss out.

- Embrace the Atmosphere: Immerse yourself in the festive spirit of Salzburg's local events, interacting with locals, sampling regional delicacies, and enjoying the unique ambiance.

- Support Local Artisans and Producers: Purchase souvenirs, crafts, and food from local vendors, contributing to the community and experiencing authentic Salzburg.

- Be Respectful: Observe local customs and etiquette, especially during religious or traditional events. Dress modestly and avoid disruptive behavior.

By participating in Salzburg's local events and festivals, you'll gain a deeper appreciation for the city's vibrant community life, its rich traditions, and its enduring cultural heritage. These gatherings offer a unique opportunity to connect with locals, experience authentic Salzburg, and create lasting memories that will enrich your journey.

Hiking and Biking Trails

Salzburg's allure extends beyond its cultural riches, encompassing a breathtaking natural landscape that beckons outdoor enthusiasts to explore its trails and immerse themselves in its scenic beauty. Whether you're a seasoned hiker seeking challenging climbs or a leisurely cyclist seeking gentle paths, Salzburg offers a diverse network of trails catering to all skill levels and preferences. Let's lace up our boots and hop on our bikes as we venture into the heart of Salzburg's natural playground.

Hiking Trails:

- Mönchsberg: This verdant hill, overlooking the city, offers a network of trails that wind through forests, meadows, and historic landmarks. The Mönchsberg Lift provides a convenient ascent, while those seeking a more active experience can hike up from the Old Town. The trails offer stunning views of Salzburg and the surrounding mountains, making it a popular choice for both locals and visitors.

- Kapuzinerberg: Another scenic hill overlooking Salzburg, Kapuzinerberg offers a more challenging hike with steeper trails and rocky terrain. The reward is equally impressive, with panoramic vistas of the city, the Salzach River, and the distant Alps. The Capuchin Monastery, perched atop the hill, adds a touch of historical charm to the experience.

- Gaisberg: For those seeking a more strenuous hike, Gaisberg, a mountain overlooking Salzburg, offers a variety of trails catering to different fitness levels. The summit rewards hikers with breathtaking 360-degree views of the city, the surrounding mountains, and the Salzkammergut Lake District.

- Untersberg: This majestic mountain, straddling the border between Austria and Germany, offers a challenging yet rewarding hike for experienced trekkers. The summit, accessible via a cable car or a strenuous hike, provides unparalleled views of the Alps and the surrounding landscape.

- Hellbrunner Allee: This picturesque avenue, lined with ancient trees and Baroque statues, offers a leisurely stroll through a historic landscape. The path leads to Hellbrunn Palace and its enchanting trick fountains, making it a popular choice for families and couples.

Biking Trails:

- Salzach River Path: This scenic path follows the Salzach River, offering stunning views of the city and its landmarks. The route is mostly flat and well-maintained, making it suitable for cyclists of all levels.

- Tauern Cycle Path: This long-distance cycle route traverses the Salzburger Land region, offering a challenging yet rewarding adventure for experienced cyclists. The path winds through picturesque valleys, along sparkling rivers, and past charming villages, showcasing the region's natural beauty and cultural heritage.

- Salzkammergut Cycle Path: This circular route explores the Salzkammergut Lake District, a UNESCO World Heritage site renowned for its pristine lakes and stunning scenery. The path offers a mix of gentle hills and flat stretches, making it suitable for cyclists of varying abilities.

- Mozart Cycle Path: This themed route connects several locations associated with Mozart's life and music, offering a unique way to experience the composer's legacy. The path winds through the city center and the surrounding countryside, showcasing Salzburg's cultural and natural treasures.

Tips for Outdoor Enthusiasts:

- Plan your route: Research the different trails and choose one that suits your fitness level and preferences.
- Check the weather: Mountain weather can be unpredictable, so check the forecast before heading out.
- Dress appropriately: Wear comfortable clothing and sturdy shoes suitable for hiking or biking.
- Pack essentials: Bring water, snacks, sunscreen, insect repellent, and a first-aid kit.
- Respect nature: Stay on designated trails, avoid disturbing wildlife, and pack out all trash.
- Enjoy the journey: Take your time to appreciate the scenery, breathe in the fresh air, and savor the experience of being in nature.

Salzburg's hiking and biking trails offer a gateway to a world of natural beauty and outdoor adventure. Whether you're seeking a challenging climb, a leisurely stroll, or a scenic bike ride, you'll find a trail that suits your interests and abilities. Embrace the opportunity to explore Salzburg's stunning landscapes and create unforgettable memories in the heart of the Alps.

Day Trips to Hidden Gems

While Salzburg itself is a treasure trove of experiences, its surroundings beckon with a collection of lesser-known destinations that offer unique encounters and breathtaking natural beauty. Venture beyond the city limits and discover hidden gems that will leave you captivated by their charm and serenity.

1. Fuschl am See: A Tranquil Lakeside Retreat

Nestled on the shores of the picturesque Fuschlsee, this idyllic village exudes a sense of peace and tranquility. Stroll along the lakeside promenade, rent a boat to explore the crystal-clear waters, or hike through the surrounding hills for panoramic views. The Schloss Fuschl, a luxurious hotel perched on a peninsula, adds a touch of grandeur to the landscape.

2. Werfen and the Eisriesenwelt Ice Caves:

Combine history and natural wonder with a visit to Werfen, a charming medieval town dominated by the imposing Hohenwerfen Fortress. Take a guided tour of the fortress, witness its spectacular falconry displays, and enjoy breathtaking views of the surrounding valley. Then, venture into the depths of the Eisriesenwelt, the world's largest ice caves, marveling at their frozen sculptures and ethereal beauty.

3. St. Gilgen and the Zwölferhorn:

This picturesque village on the shores of the Wolfgangsee, Mozart's mother's birthplace, offers a charming blend of history, culture, and natural beauty. Stroll through its narrow streets, visit the Mozart Haus museum, and take a scenic cable car ride to the summit of the Zwölferhorn for panoramic views of the lake and surrounding mountains.

4. Golling Waterfall and the Bluntautal Valley:

Immerse yourself in the raw power and beauty of nature with a visit to the Golling Waterfall, a cascading torrent that plunges 75 meters into a dramatic gorge. Hike through the surrounding Bluntautal Valley, a lush green oasis with hiking trails, waterfalls, and hidden swimming spots.

5. Mattsee: A Hidden Gem on the Lake

Escape the crowds and discover the tranquil beauty of Mattsee, a charming town nestled on the shores of a picturesque lake. Explore its historic center, visit the Mattsee Abbey, and enjoy a leisurely boat ride or swim in the lake's refreshing waters.

Tips for Day Trips:

- Plan your transportation: Research the best way to reach your chosen destination, whether by public transportation, organized tour, or rental car.
- Pack essentials: Bring water, snacks, sunscreen, comfortable shoes, and a camera to capture the memories.
- Check opening hours: Confirm the opening hours of attractions and plan your itinerary accordingly.
- Embrace spontaneity: Allow room for serendipitous encounters and unexpected discoveries.
- Savor the moment: Take your time to appreciate the unique beauty and atmosphere of each destination.

These hidden gems, each with its own distinct charm and allure, offer a refreshing alternative to Salzburg's more popular tourist attractions. By venturing off the beaten path, you'll discover a side of the region that's often overlooked, creating a more personalized and enriching travel experience.

209 | SALZBURG TRAVEL GUIDE 2025

210 | SALZBURG TRAVEL GUIDE 2025

CHAPTER 10

Salzburg Travel Resources

Useful Websites and Apps

In today's digital age, a wealth of online resources can empower travelers to plan, navigate, and enhance their Salzburg experience. From official tourism websites and interactive maps to specialized apps and social media platforms, these digital tools provide valuable information, practical tips, and inspiration for your journey.

Official Tourism Websites:

- Salzburg Tourism: The official website of Salzburg Tourism is a comprehensive resource for planning your trip. It offers information on attractions, events, accommodations, transportation, and more.

- Visit Salzburg: This website provides additional insights into Salzburg's cultural offerings, including festivals, concerts, and exhibitions.

- Austria Tourism: The official website of Austria Tourism provides general information about traveling to Austria, including visa and entry requirements, transportation options, and regional highlights.

Navigation and Transportation Apps:

- Google Maps: This indispensable app provides detailed maps, real-time traffic updates, and public transportation schedules for Salzburg and its surroundings.

- ÖBB Scotty: The official app of the Austrian Federal Railways (ÖBB) allows you to plan and book train journeys, check schedules, and purchase tickets.

- Salzburg Verkehr: This app provides information on Salzburg's public transportation network, including bus and trolleybus routes, schedules, and real-time updates.

- Qando Salzburg: This app offers a convenient way to purchase tickets for public transportation, as well as access to discounts and special offers.

Specialized Apps:

- Salzburg Card App: If you purchase the Salzburg Card, download the accompanying app for easy access to information on included attractions, discounts, and special offers.

- Sound of Music Guide: This app provides a self-guided tour of the film's iconic locations in and around Salzburg, including audio commentary and historical insights.

- Salzburg Museum App: This app enhances your visit to the Salzburg Museum with additional information, interactive features, and audio guides.

- Salzburg Festival App: This app provides up-to-date information on festival events, schedules, and ticket availability.

Social Media and Online Communities:

- Instagram: Follow Salzburg Tourism and other local accounts on Instagram for stunning photos and inspiration for your trip. Use hashtags like #Salzburg and #VisitSalzburg to discover hidden gems and connect with fellow travelers.

- Facebook: Join Salzburg-related Facebook groups and pages to connect with locals and other travelers, get insider tips, and stay informed about upcoming events.

- TripAdvisor: Read reviews and recommendations from other travelers on attractions, restaurants, accommodations, and activities in Salzburg.

- Blogs and Travel Websites: Numerous blogs and travel websites offer valuable insights and firsthand experiences of Salzburg. Search for keywords like "Salzburg travel blog" or "Salzburg hidden gems" to discover a wealth of information.

Additional Tips:

- Download offline maps: Ensure you have access to maps even without an internet connection by downloading offline maps of Salzburg and the surrounding region.

- Utilize free Wi-Fi: Take advantage of free Wi-Fi available at many cafes, restaurants, and public spaces to stay connected and access online resources.

- Stay updated: Check official websites and social media pages for the latest information on attractions, events, and transportation options.

- Use translation tools: If you encounter language barriers, use translation apps or websites to communicate with locals and understand signs and menus.

- Embrace the digital age: Technology can enhance your travel experience, but don't forget to disconnect and savor the moment. Put your phone away and immerse yourself in the beauty and culture of Salzburg.

By utilizing these valuable online resources and apps, you can streamline your travel planning, navigate the city with ease, and uncover hidden gems that might otherwise go unnoticed. Embrace the digital age and let technology enhance your Salzburg adventure, allowing you to focus on creating unforgettable memories in this enchanting city.

Local Tour Operators and Guides

For those seeking organized tours and personalized experiences, Salzburg boasts a selection of reputable tour operators and knowledgeable guides who can unlock the city's hidden treasures and provide enriching insights into its history, culture, and natural beauty. Let's explore some of the most recommended options to enhance your Salzburg adventure:

Panorama Tours:

- **Overview**: A leading tour operator in Salzburg, Panorama Tours offers a wide range of guided excursions, from city walks and Sound of Music tours to day trips to the surrounding regions. Their experienced guides, fluent in multiple languages, provide informative and engaging commentary, ensuring a memorable experience.

- **Recommended Tours**:

- **Original Sound of Music Tour:** Relive the magic of the iconic film with this comprehensive tour that visits key filming locations, including Mirabell Gardens, Leopoldskron Palace, and Mondsee Abbey.

- **Salzburg City Walk:** Discover the highlights of Salzburg's Old Town on a guided walking tour, exploring its charming streets, historic landmarks, and architectural gems.

- **Eagle's Nest Tour:** Venture into the Bavarian Alps and visit the historic Eagle's Nest, perched atop the Kehlstein mountain, for breathtaking panoramic views.

- **Hallstatt Day Trip:** Escape to the picturesque lakeside village of Hallstatt, a UNESCO World Heritage site, and immerse yourself in its timeless beauty and tranquil atmosphere.

Bob's Special Tours:

- **Overview:** Bob's Special Tours offers personalized and intimate experiences, focusing on small group sizes and customized itineraries. Their knowledgeable guides, passionate about Salzburg's history and culture, provide a unique and insightful perspective on the city.

- **Recommended Tours:**

    o **Private City Tour:** Tailor your Salzburg experience with a private city tour, focusing on your specific interests and preferences.

    o **Salzburg Food Tour:** Embark on a culinary adventure, sampling local specialties and discovering hidden gems with a passionate foodie guide.

    o **Hidden Salzburg Walk:** Venture off the beaten path and explore Salzburg's lesser-known neighborhoods, uncovering their authentic charm and local secrets.

    o **Mozart City Tour:** Delve into the life and legacy of Mozart with this specialized tour that visits key sites associated with the composer.

Salzburg Guides:

- **Overview**: Salzburg Guides is a collective of independent, licensed guides who offer a range of personalized tours and experiences. Their expertise spans various fields, including history, art, music, and nature, ensuring a tailored experience based on your interests.

- **Recommended Guides and Tours:**

- o **Marcus A**: This highly-rated guide offers engaging and informative tours of Salzburg's Old Town, Hohensalzburg Fortress, and surrounding areas.

- o **Michaela M.**: Specializing in personalized experiences, Michaela offers customized tours tailored to your interests, from art and architecture to music and gastronomy.

- o **Michael T.**: A passionate outdoorsman, Michael leads scenic hikes and bike tours in the Salzburg region, showcasing its natural beauty and hidden trails.

Additional Resources:

- **ToursByLocals**: This platform connects travelers with local guides who offer a variety of personalized tours and experiences in Salzburg.

- **GetYourGuide**: This online platform provides a wide selection of tours and activities in Salzburg, from city walks and Sound of Music tours to day trips and outdoor adventures.

- **Viator**: Another popular platform for booking tours and activities, Viator offers a diverse range of options in Salzburg, catering to different interests and budgets.

Tips for Choosing a Tour or Guide:

- Research and Compare: Take the time to research different tour operators and guides, reading reviews and comparing offerings to find the best fit for your interests and budget.

- Consider Group Size: If you prefer a more intimate experience, opt for a small group tour or a private guide.

- Check Credentials: Ensure your chosen guide is licensed and knowledgeable about Salzburg's history, culture, and attractions.

- Ask Questions: Don't hesitate to ask questions about the tour itinerary, inclusions, and any specific interests you have.

- Book in Advance: During peak season, tours and guides can book up quickly. Secure your reservations well in advance to avoid disappointment.

By choosing a reputable tour operator or guide, you can enhance your Salzburg experience with expert insights, personalized attention, and unforgettable memories. Whether you're seeking a comprehensive overview of the city, a deep dive into its cultural treasures, or an outdoor adventure in its breathtaking surroundings, these curated experiences will unlock the magic of

Salzburg and leave you with a profound appreciation for its timeless allure.

Emergency Contact Information

While Salzburg is generally a safe city, it's always wise to be prepared for any unforeseen circumstances. Here's a list of essential emergency contact information to ensure you have access to help when you need it most:

Emergency Numbers:

- European Emergency Number: 112 (This number will connect you to the appropriate emergency service, including police, ambulance, or fire brigade)

- Police: 133

- Ambulance: 144

- Fire Department: 122

Hospitals:

- Landeskrankenhaus Salzburg (SALK): This is the main public hospital in Salzburg, offering a wide range of medical services and emergency care.

    o Address: Müllner Hauptstraße 48, 5020 Salzburg

    o Phone: +43 662 4482 0

- Universitätsklinikum Salzburg (University Hospital Salzburg): Another major hospital in Salzburg, providing specialized medical care and emergency services.
  - Address: Ignaz-Harrer-Straße 79, 5020 Salzburg
  - Phone: +43 5 7255-0
- Krankenhaus der Barmherzigen Brüder Salzburg: This private hospital offers a range of medical services, including emergency care.
  - Address: Kajetanerplatz 1, 5020 Salzburg
  - Phone: +43 662 80880

Embassies and Consulates:

- Your Country's Embassy/Consulate: It's advisable to have the contact information for your country's embassy or consulate in Austria readily available. They can provide assistance in case of lost or stolen passports, legal issues, or other emergencies. You can find a list of embassies and consulates in Austria on the website of the Austrian Federal Ministry for European and International Affairs.

Other Important Contacts:

- Medical On-Call Service: 141 (This number connects you to an on-call doctor for non-emergency medical advice and assistance)

- Dental Emergency Service: +43 662 8088 5100 (Available evenings and weekends)

- Pharmacy On-Call Service: 1455 (This number provides information on the nearest open pharmacy)

- Salzburg Tourism Information: +43 662 88987-0 (For general tourist information and assistance)

Additional Tips:

- Travel Insurance: Ensure you have comprehensive travel insurance that covers medical emergencies, trip cancellations, and lost or stolen belongings.

- Carry Important Documents: Keep copies of your passport, visa, travel insurance, and other essential documents in a separate location from the originals.

- Register with Your Embassy: If your country has an embassy or consulate in Austria, consider registering your travel plans with them. This can be helpful in case of emergencies or natural disasters.

- Learn Basic German Phrases: Knowing a few basic German phrases, such as "Ich brauche einen Arzt" (I need a doctor) or "Ich habe mein Passport verloren" (I lost my passport), can be helpful in emergency situations.

- Stay Informed: Be aware of your surroundings and follow local news and advisories, especially during severe weather or other potential emergencies.

By having these essential emergency contact numbers and information readily available, you can ensure a safe and worry-free visit to Salzburg. Remember, preparation is key to handling any unexpected situations that may arise during your travels.

Additional Tips and Advice

Beyond the essential practicalities, here are some final insights and suggestions to ensure a smooth, enjoyable, and enriching trip to Salzburg:

Embrace the Local Culture:

- Immerse yourself in the language: Even a few basic German phrases can go a long way in connecting with locals and experiencing the culture more authentically.

- Respect local customs: Familiarize yourself with Austrian etiquette and traditions to ensure respectful interactions and avoid any unintentional faux pas.

- Attend local events: Participate in festivals, markets, and community gatherings to experience Salzburg's vibrant spirit and connect with its residents.

Explore Beyond the City Center:

- Discover hidden gems: Venture off the beaten path to uncover Salzburg's lesser-known neighborhoods, charming villages, and scenic landscapes.

- Take day trips: The surrounding region offers a wealth of natural beauty and cultural attractions. Consider exploring the Salzkammergut Lake District, the Berchtesgaden National Park, or the picturesque town of Hallstatt.

Savor the Culinary Delights:

- Sample local specialties: Indulge in traditional Austrian dishes like Wiener Schnitzel, Tafelspitz, and Salzburger Nockerl.

- Visit local markets: Explore the vibrant farmers' markets and discover fresh produce, regional specialties, and artisanal products.

- Enjoy a coffeehouse experience: Embrace the Viennese coffeehouse culture, a UNESCO-listed intangible cultural heritage, and savor a leisurely afternoon with coffee and cake.

Embrace the Arts and Culture:

- Attend a performance: Experience the magic of live music, theater, or opera at one of Salzburg's many cultural venues.

- Visit museums and galleries: Explore the city's rich artistic heritage through its diverse museums and galleries, from the Salzburg Museum to contemporary art spaces.

- Participate in workshops or classes: Learn a new skill or deepen your appreciation for a particular art form by attending a workshop or class.

Practical Tips:

- Pack light: Salzburg is a walkable city, so pack light to avoid lugging heavy bags around.

- Wear comfortable shoes: You'll likely be doing a lot of walking, so choose footwear that provides good support.

- Stay hydrated: Carry a reusable water bottle and refill it throughout the day to stay hydrated, especially during warmer months.

- Use sunscreen and insect repellent: Protect yourself from the sun's rays and pesky insects, particularly during outdoor activities.

- Be prepared for the weather: Salzburg's weather can be unpredictable, so pack layers and be prepared for rain or shine.

Embrace the Unexpected:

- Allow for spontaneity: While it's helpful to have a plan, be open to serendipitous encounters and unexpected discoveries.

- Get lost in the moment: Put away your phone and maps, and simply wander through the city's streets, absorbing its atmosphere and charm.

- Connect with locals: Strike up conversations with locals, ask for recommendations, and gain insights into their way of life.

Most importantly, remember to relax, enjoy the journey, and savor every moment of your Salzburg adventure. This enchanting city, with its rich history, vibrant culture, and stunning natural beauty, promises to leave a lasting impression on your heart and soul.

227 | S A L Z B U R G   T R A V E L   G U I D E   2 0 2 5

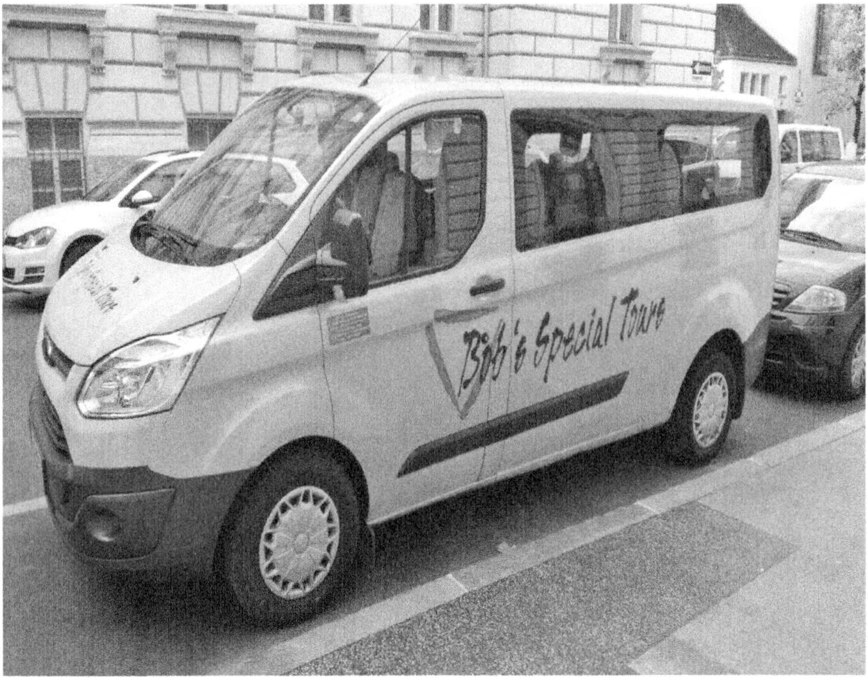
Bob's Special Tours

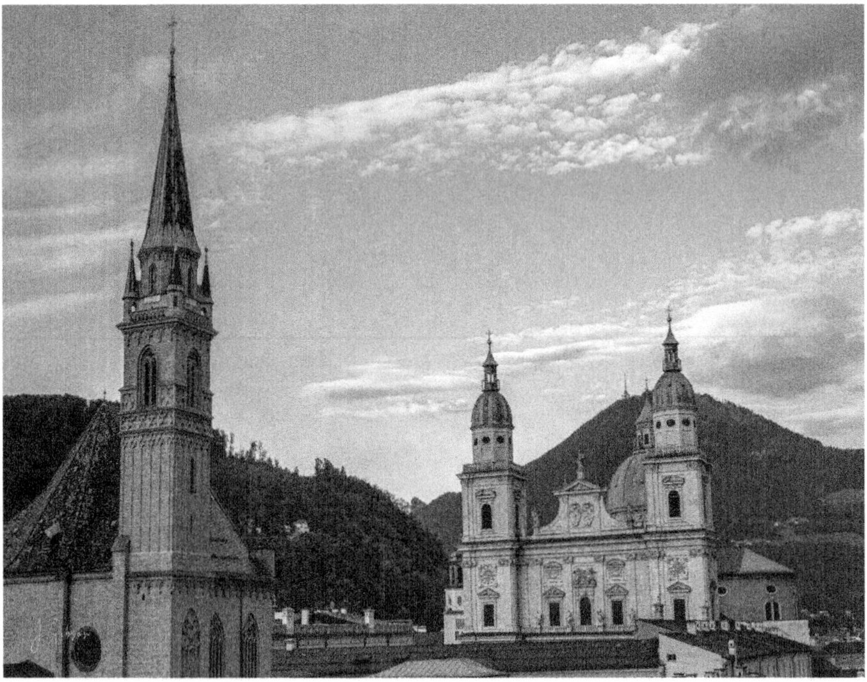

CONCLUSION

Reflect on the magic of Salzburg

As your Salzburg adventure draws to a close, the echoes of its enchanting melodies, historical whispers, and breathtaking vistas will undoubtedly linger in your heart and soul. This city, where music and magic intertwine, has woven a tapestry of experiences that will forever color your memories and inspire your wanderlust.

From the majestic Hohensalzburg Fortress, standing sentinel over the city for centuries, to the delicate beauty of Mirabell Gardens, where romance blooms amidst Baroque splendor, Salzburg's landmarks have etched themselves into your consciousness. The footsteps of Mozart, echoing through his birthplace and residence, have resonated with your own creative spirit, while the hidden gems nestled within its charming neighborhoods have revealed a side of the city that few visitors get to experience.

The vibrant festivals, from the world-renowned Salzburg Festival to the intimate Mozart Week, have filled your ears with harmonious melodies and your heart with cultural enrichment. The playful trick fountains of Hellbrunn Palace have ignited your childlike wonder, while the serene beauty of the Salzburg Lake

District and the Bavarian Alps has rejuvenated your soul amidst nature's grandeur.

Salzburg is a city that transcends time, its rich history and cultural heritage intertwined with its vibrant present. Its Baroque architecture, its musical legacy, and its natural beauty create an ambiance that is both captivating and inspiring, leaving an indelible mark on all who venture within its embrace.

As you bid farewell to this enchanting city, carry with you the cherished memories you've created, the friendships you've forged, and the lessons you've learned. Salzburg's magic will forever reside within you, a gentle reminder of the beauty, wonder, and possibility that await in the world. May your journey continue to unfold with the same spirit of adventure, curiosity, and appreciation for the extraordinary that you discovered in Mozart's city.

Farewell, Salzburg, until we meet again. Your melodies will forever echo in our hearts, your landscapes will forever grace our dreams, and your spirit will forever inspire our wanderlust.

Encourage exploration and discovery

While this guidebook has unveiled Salzburg's treasures, remember that the true magic of travel lies in the unexpected discoveries and serendipitous encounters that await beyond its pages. Embrace the spirit of adventure, step off the well-trodden path, and allow Salzburg to surprise and delight you in its own unique way.

Wander through its labyrinthine streets, guided by your curiosity and intuition. Stumble upon hidden courtyards, tucked-away cafes, and charming shops that beckon with their unique offerings. Strike up conversations with locals, listen to their stories, and gain insights into their way of life.

Attend a spontaneous concert in a hidden church, savor a picnic lunch in a secluded park, or simply sit by the Salzach River and watch the world go by. These unscripted moments, often the most cherished, will weave themselves into the tapestry of your Salzburg experience, creating memories that will last a lifetime.

Remember, Salzburg is not just a destination; it's a journey of exploration and discovery. Let its beauty, its history, and its vibrant culture ignite your imagination and inspire your wanderlust. Embrace the unexpected, follow your heart, and create your own unforgettable Salzburg story.

As you venture forth, remember that this guidebook is merely a starting point. It's a compass to guide you through the city's highlights, but the true adventure lies in forging your own path, uncovering hidden gems, and embracing the serendipitous moments that make travel so rewarding.

So, step outside your comfort zone, let your curiosity lead the way, and allow Salzburg to surprise and delight you. The possibilities are endless, and the memories you create will be uniquely yours.

Final tips and farewell

As you embark on your journey to Salzburg, may this guidebook serve as a trusted companion, illuminating its hidden treasures, inspiring your explorations, and fostering a deeper connection to its vibrant spirit. May you embrace the unexpected, savor the serendipitous moments, and create memories that will forever bind you to this enchanting city.

Salzburg, with its timeless allure and harmonious blend of history, culture, and natural beauty, awaits your arrival. Its melodies will resonate in your heart, its landscapes will paint vivid pictures in your mind, and its people will welcome you with open arms.

So go forth, intrepid traveler, and let Salzburg's magic unfold before you. May your journey be filled with joy, wonder, and a profound appreciation for the extraordinary.

Auf Wiedersehen, and until we meet again in Mozart's city!

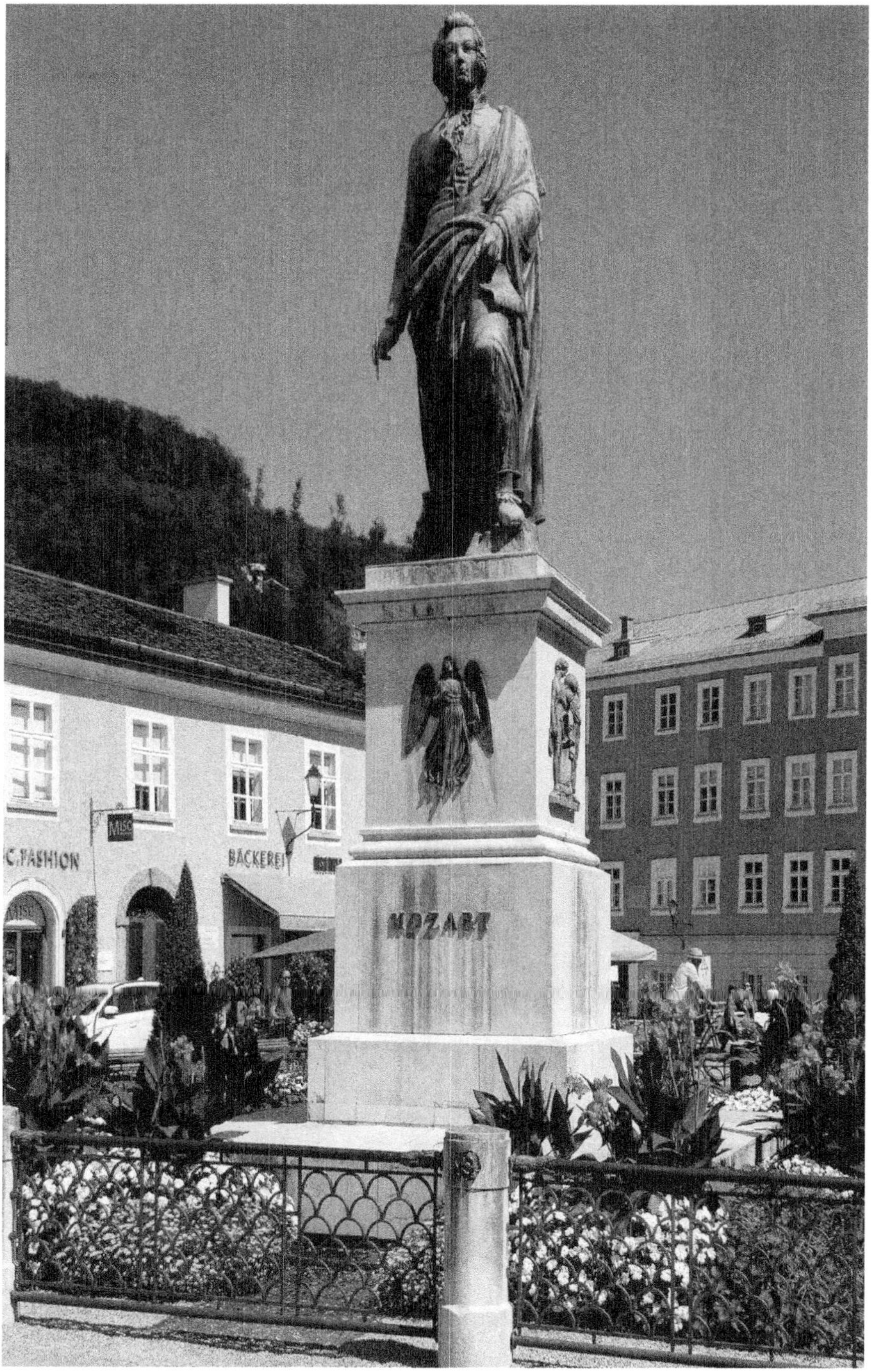
C.FASHION
BÄCKEREI
MOZART

A Heartfelt Thank You

Dear Reader,

From the bottom of my heart, thank you for choosing this Salzburg Travel Guide to accompany you on your Austrian adventure. It's been a joy to share my passion for this enchanting city with you, and I sincerely hope this book has sparked your excitement and equipped you to create unforgettable memories.

Your feedback is invaluable to me. If you've enjoyed this guide, please consider leaving a rating or review on Amazon. Your kind words not only encourage me as an author but also help fellow travelers discover the magic of Salzburg. Whether it's a quick star rating or a detailed review, your thoughts matter.

Thank you again for your support, and I wish you a truly wonderful journey to Mozart's city!

With warmest regards,

Diane F. Thompson

235 | SALZBURG TRAVEL GUIDE 2025

236 | SALZBURG TRAVEL GUIDE 2025

237 | SALZBURG TRAVEL GUIDE 2025

238 | SALZBURG TRAVEL GUIDE 2025

239 | SALZBURG TRAVEL GUIDE 2025

240 | SALZBURG TRAVEL GUIDE 2025

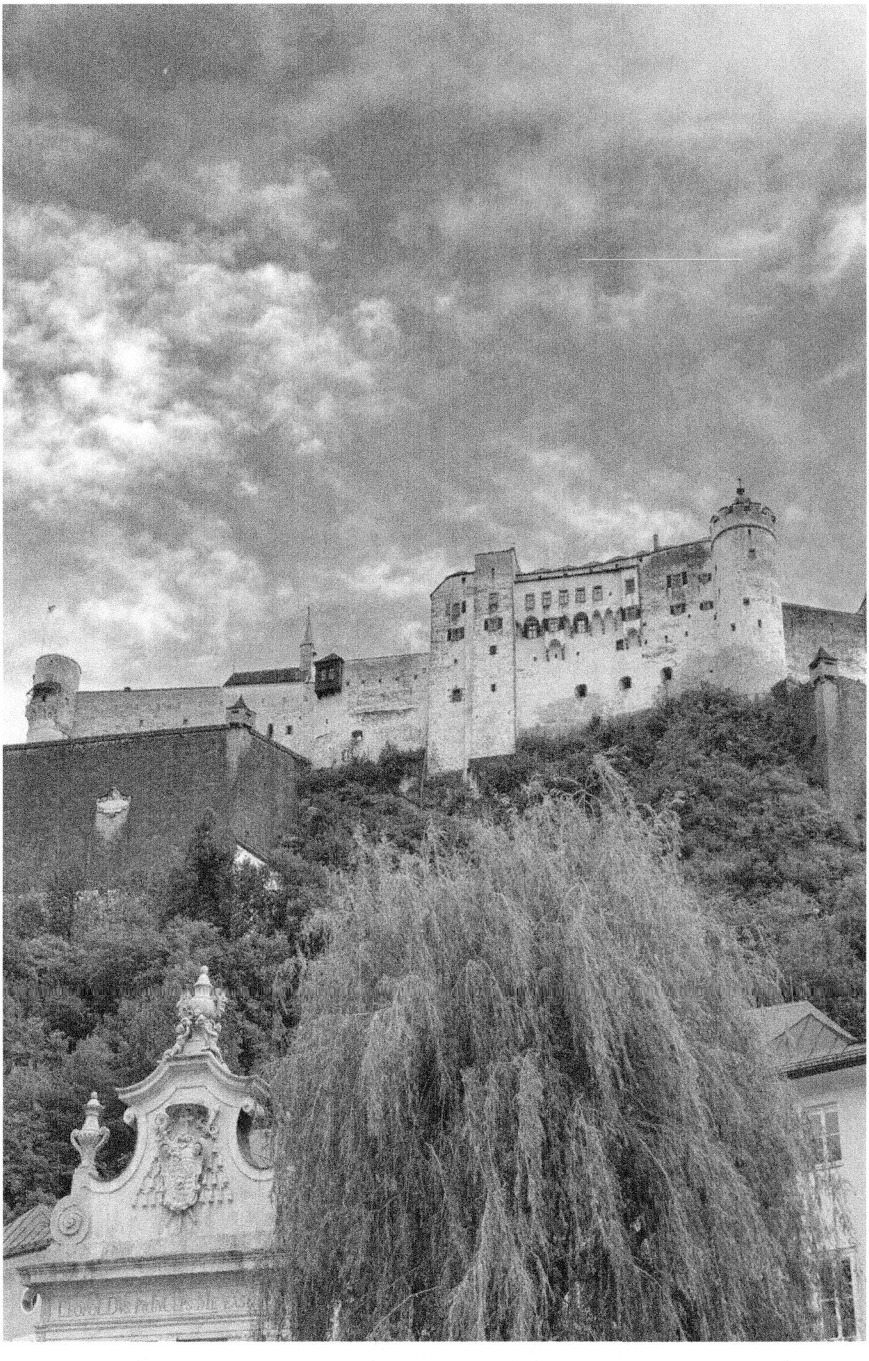

242 | SALZBURG TRAVEL GUIDE 2025

243 | SALZBURG TRAVEL GUIDE 2025

244 | SALZBURG TRAVEL GUIDE 2025

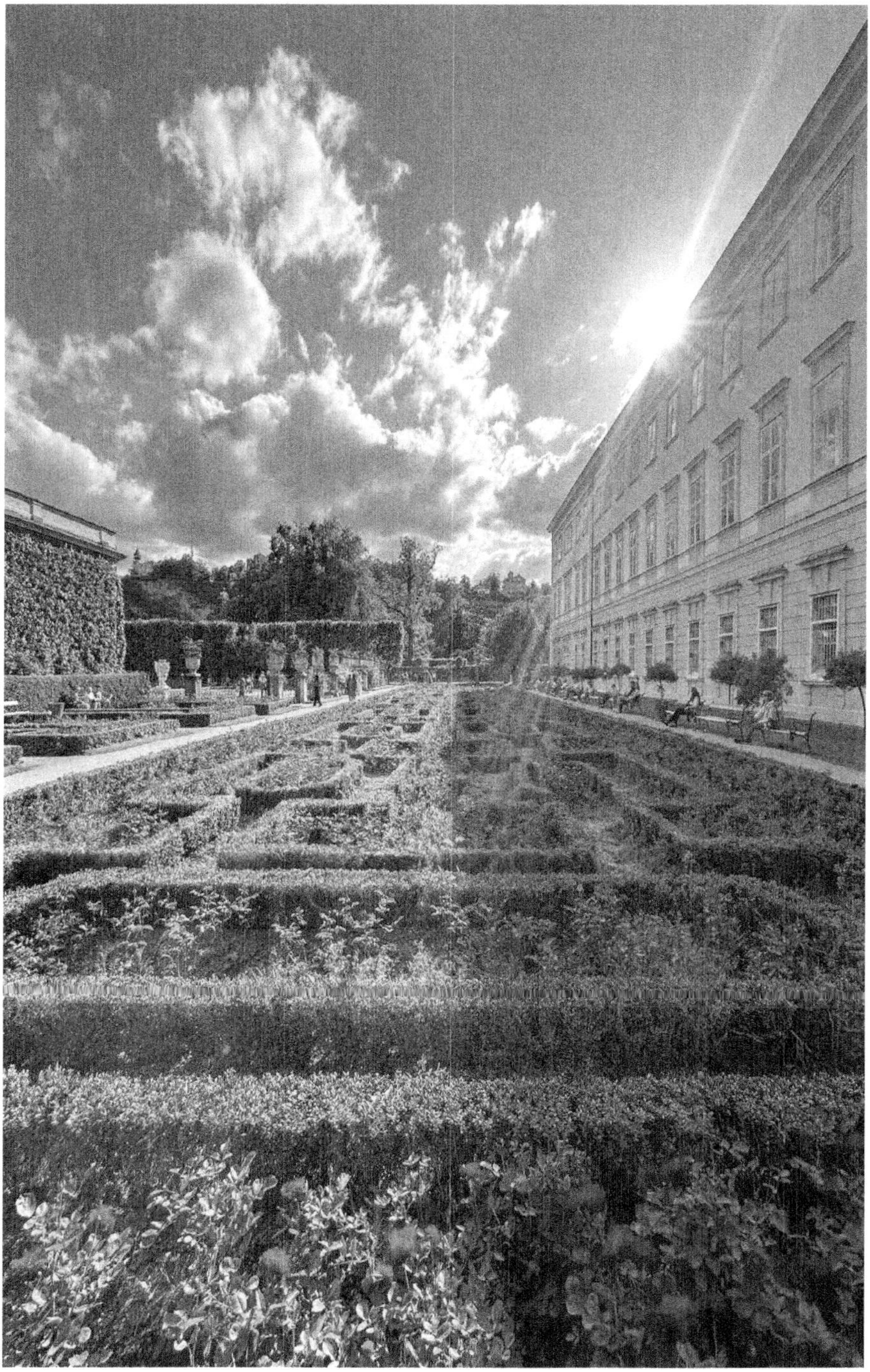

246 | SALZBURG TRAVEL GUIDE 2025

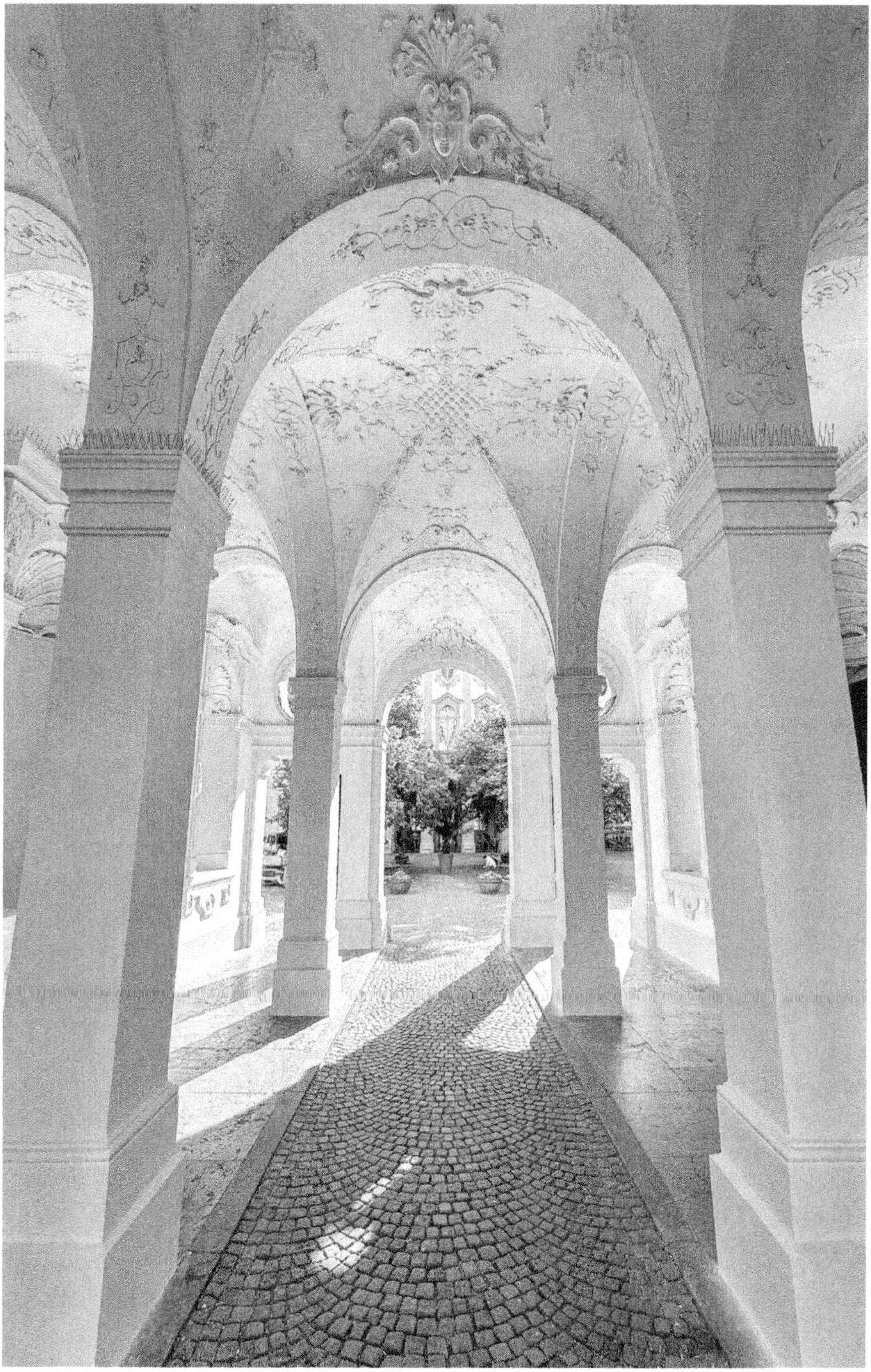

248|SALZBURG TRAVEL GUIDE 2025

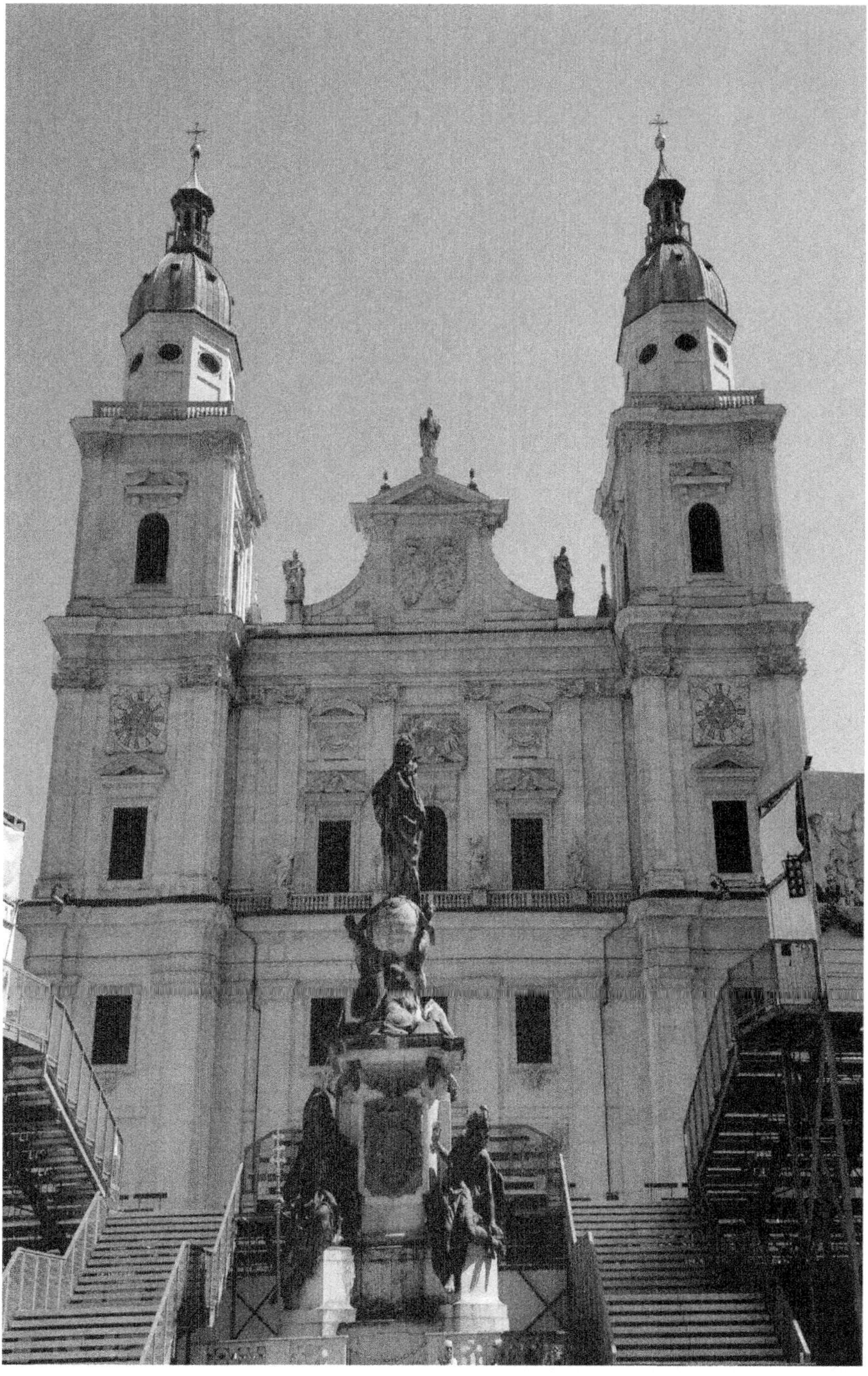

250 | SALZBURG TRAVEL GUIDE 2025

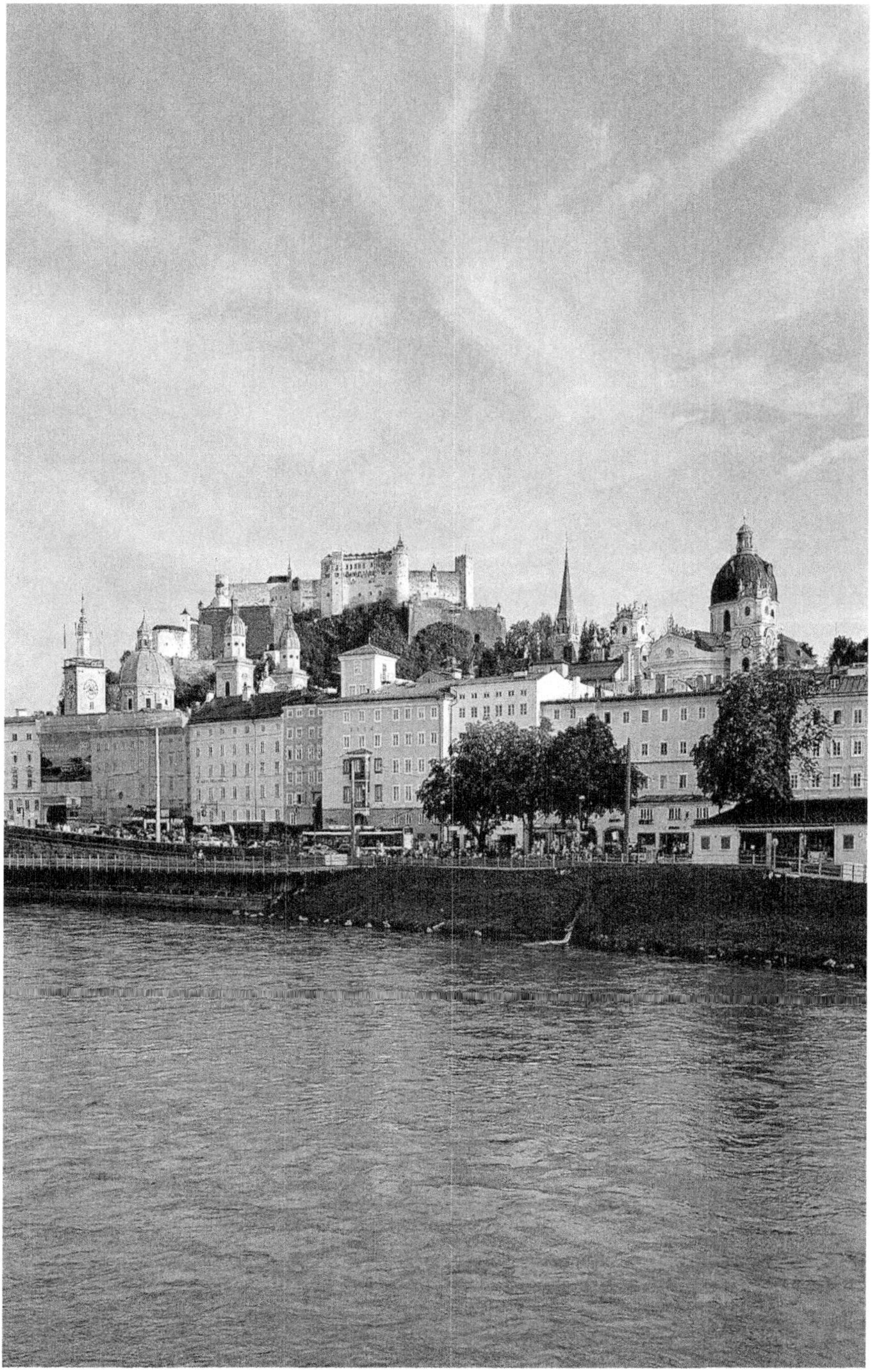

252 | SALZBURG TRAVEL GUIDE 2025

253 | SALZBURG TRAVEL GUIDE 2025

254 | SALZBURG TRAVEL GUIDE 2025

255 | SALZBURG TRAVEL GUIDE 2025

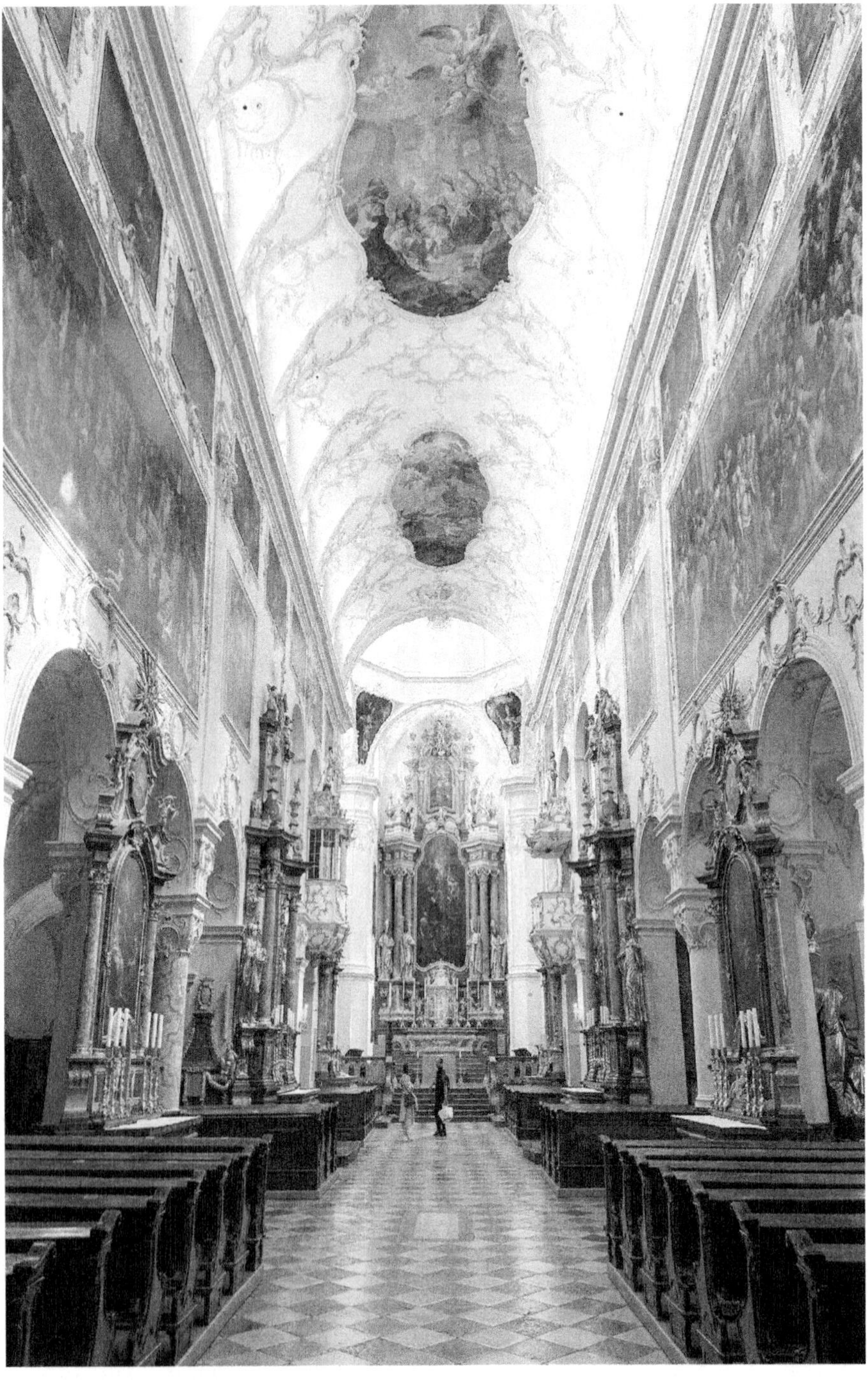

257 | SALZBURG TRAVEL GUIDE 2025

258 | SALZBURG TRAVEL GUIDE 2025

Travel Itinerary

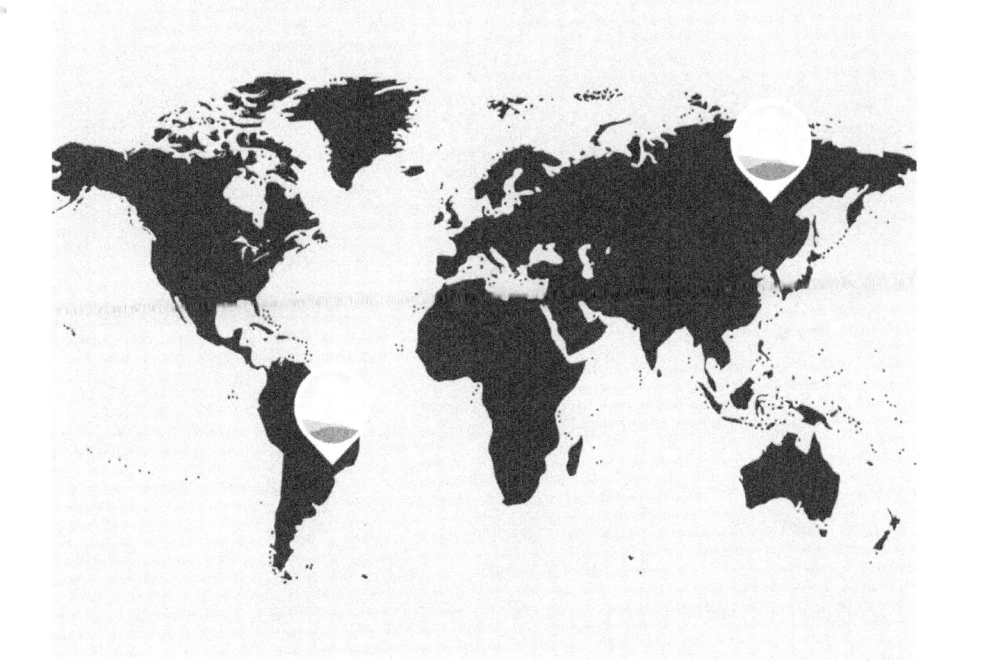

Date:

Location:

Budget:

KINDS OF TRANSPORTATION:

My Travel Planner
Personal Itinerary

TODAY'S LOG

- 6 AM
- 7 AM
- 8 AM
- 9 AM
- 10 AM
- 11 AM
- 12 PM
- 1 PM
- 2 PM
- 3 PM
- 4 PM
- 5 PM
- 6 PM

PLACES TO GO

LOCAL FOODS TO TRY

REMINDER

Date:

Location:

Budget:

KINDS OF TRANSPORTATION:

My Travel Planner
Personal Itinerary

TODAY'S LOG

6 AM	
7 AM	
8 AM	
9 AM	
10 AM	
11 AM	
12 PM	
1 PM	
2 PM	
3 PM	
4 PM	
5 PM	
6 PM	

PLACES TO GO

LOCAL FOODS TO TRY

REMINDER

261 | SALZBURG TRAVEL GUIDE 2025

Date:

Location:

Budget:

KINDS OF TRANSPORTATION:

My Travel Planner
Personal Itinerary

TODAY'S LOG

| 6 AM |
| 7 AM |
| 8 AM |
| 9 AM |
| 10 AM |
| 11 AM |
| 12 PM |
| 1 PM |
| 2 PM |
| 3 PM |
| 4 PM |
| 5 PM |
| 6 PM |

PLACES TO GO

LOCAL FOODS TO TRY

REMINDER

262 | SALZBURG TRAVEL GUIDE 2025

Date:

Location:

Budget:

KINDS OF TRANSPORTATION:

My Travel Planner
Personal Itinerary

TODAY'S LOG

6 AM
7 AM
8 AM
9 AM
10 AM
11 AM
12 PM
1 PM
2 PM
3 PM
4 PM
5 PM
6 PM

PLACES TO GO

LOCAL FOODS TO TRY

REMINDER

263 | SALZBURG TRAVEL GUIDE 2025

Date:

Location:

Budget:

KINDS OF TRANSPORTATION:

My Travel Planner
Personal Itinerary

TODAY'S LOG

Time
6 AM
7 AM
8 AM
9 AM
10 AM
11 AM
12 PM
1 PM
2 PM
3 PM
4 PM
5 PM
6 PM

PLACES TO GO

LOCAL FOODS TO TRY

REMINDER